D0991961

German Poetry
from 1750 to 1900

The German Library : Volume 39

Volkmar Sander, General Editor

GERMAN POETRY
from 1750 to 1900

Edited by Robert M. Browning

Foreword by Michael Hamburger

CONTINUUM · NEW YORK

1984

The Continuum Publishing Company
370 Lexington Avenue, New York, NY 10017

Printed in the United States of America

Library of Congress Cataloging in Publication Data

Main entry under title:

German poetry from 1750–1900

(The German library; v. 39)
English and German.
Includes index.
1. German poetry—19th century—Translations into
English. 2. English poetry—Translations from German.
3. German poetry—19th century. I. Browning,
Robert Marcellus, 1911–   . II. Series.
PT1160.E5G42 1984   830'.8   83-23980
ISBN 0-8264-0282-8
ISBN 0-8264-0283-6 (pbk.)

Acknowledgments will be found on page 279,
which constitutes an extension of the copyright page.

Contents

Contents · ix

Foreword

The contents of this anthology are drawn from a long period in German literature, and a period packed with the most various and contradictory developments. Some of these can be understood without much difficulty by readers unfamiliar with the historical background, because they have rough parallels in the English-language poetry of the same period. Others are peculiar to the German-language poetry produced in the many separate states that made up Germany before its unification, in Austria, and in Switzerland. To comment on the differences between the literatures of those three regions alone—when Austria included Hungary and many of the Slav peoples—is beyond my scope here, but a few generalizations about German peculiarities may be helpful.

One thing that must be borne in mind is that Germany was not a nation until the end of the period covered by the anthology—and even then Bavaria remained a separate kingdom. This political fact has a bearing on the literary developments. Because Germany had no capital city and no national institutions, it had no classical literature comparable to that of the "Augustan" period in English literature. Hence the belated "Weimar" classicism of the late eighteenth century—an almost deliberate attempt by Goethe and Schiller to create the missing literature. Hence also the concurrence of Romantic and classical trends at that time—a concurrence so confusing to non-German readers as to be almost incomprehensible. That is why Goethe and Schiller—the very creators of that belated classicism—are often regarded as Romantics by English and American critics. What is more, Goethe's "Weimar" classicism was only one phase in his development, and Schiller, too, had passed through a politically and stylistically revolutionary phase quite inimical to classicism. Some of Goethe's poetry is pre-Romantic, some of it is Romantic—by British or American criteria—and some of it is post-Romantic or positively anti-Romantic, quite apart from his deliberately classicizing phase. The same difficulty of classification arises over the work of Hölderlin, a solitary and incomparable poet younger than Goethe or Schiller, close to both of them in some of his work, but quite unconnected with the early Romantic school whose beginnings were exactly contemporary both with his mature work and with Weimar classicism. In view of those complexities it may be best for non-specialists to forget all about the categories romantic and classical. German Romanticism, in any case, is not the same thing as the coeval English Romanticism of Wordsworth, Coleridge, Southey, or Scott, not to mention Blake, a poet as unclassifiable as Hölderlin. Nor is Weimar classicism the same thing as the French or British classicism of the seventeenth and early eighteenth centuries.

To understand those peculiarly German developments it is best to concentrate on two or three powerful influences on all the poetry produced by German-language writers during the whole period covered by this anthology, from the late eighteenth century to the late nineteenth. The first of these is the Christian devotional verse of earlier periods, the Protestant hymn above all, which tended to be secularized—filled with aspirations more humanistic than strictly Christian—by the late eighteenth century. The influence of French rationalism (and anti-rationalism in the case of Rousseau), of German philosophical idealism, and the social changes culminating in the French Revolution contributed to this change of content. Much of Schiller's rhymed poetry and Hölderlin's early "hymns" (not represented in this anthology) are outstanding instances of this secularization of devotional and edifying types of verse. In the work of Matthias Claudius the connection is still more apparent, because his Christian faith, combined with a desire to write in the language of common folk, made him less susceptible to the various humanistic creeds that had begun to displace the traditional gists of devotional verse. His most popular poem, *Abendlied,* links on to the devotional poetry of the seventeenth century, though its nature imagery points to the sensibility of his own age.

The second influence is that of classical poetry proper, that is Greek and Latin. Though this influence had been pervasive in European poetry for centuries, the eighteenth-century classical revival in Germany since Winckelmann had established a poetic tradition of imitation distinct from the practices of other European literatures. Before Goethe, Schiller, and Hölderlin, many German poets had written in meters directly imitated or adapted from those of the Greek and Latin poets. Klopstock's odes, for instance, were written in classical "feet," though their meters were Klopstock's own—much as Greek poets had devised meters now associated with their names. The outstanding eighteenth-century German translation of Homer, too, by Johann Heinrich Voss, was into a German form of the Greek hexameter, not the rhymed iambic couplets favored by Dryden and Pope; and even Klopstock's Christian epic, *Der Messias,* was written in classical hexameters. Hölty and Matthisson are other pre-Weimar practitioners of this kind of classicizing verse.

These formal approximations to Greek and Latin verse may seem a mere technicality, to do with the fact that German, as an inflected language, lends itself rhythmically to the adaptation of classical feet, especially dactyls; but every schoolboy knows, or ought to know, that meter and rhythm are more than technicalities, that the "how" of a poem is inseparable from its "what," its medium inseparable from its message. In practice, the formal approximation went hand in hand with a degree of identification unparalleled in the classicism or Augustanism of other modern literatures. When, in 1796, Hölderlin turned from the rhymed verse of his early "hymns" to Greek ode forms and elegiacs, that was a turning point in his development—a profession of faith, as well as a liberation from a convention he had outgrown. The same is true of Goethe's would-be imitations of Pindar in the 1770s, or his later imitation of the Latin elegiac poets in his *Roman Elegies.* Because Hölderlin's Hellenism involved the whole man, it set up a religious conflict between the Christian faith of his upbringing and a pantheism and polytheism taken over from the Greeks—a conflict fought out in his later "Pindaric" hymns, to the point of exhaustion and mental collapse; and the publication of his *Roman Elegies,* with two significant omissions, earned Goethe the reputation of being a pagan libertine. The poetry of those two incomparable writers alone is ample proof that the imitation of classical forms was meaningful only inasmuch as it was also a coming to grips with the spirit of Greece or Rome—the spirit of Greece or Rome as understood and interpreted by a modern sensibility, it goes without saying.

Although this grappling with antiquity went underground in most German poetry of the nineteenth century—with a few exceptions, such as Mörike, who shared Hölderlin's educational background of Swabian pietism combined with classical studies, and some of Rückert's prolific and many-sided work—it reemerged with a vengeance toward the end of the century, in Nietzsche. Not only by his emphasis on pre-Socratic and preclassical Greece, on the Dionysian principle in Greek culture, but also as a writer of dithyrambic free verse, Nietzsche linked on to the early poetry of Goethe and the later poetry of Hölderlin (which was scarcely known or fully available at the time). Both Goethe and Hölderlin had anticipated some of his basic discoveries and emphases, more by intuition than by the scholarship on which Nietzsche was able to draw almost a century later.

The astonishing resort to free verse by Goethe and by Hölderlin was due to a fruitful misunderstanding of Pindar's prosody, though Hölderlin continued to write free verse when he had discovered the triadic metric of Pindar's choric odes. This misunderstanding gave Goethe the perfect poetic medium for his *Sturm und Drang* verse. Pindar's seeming obscurity was his license to write a poetic "half-nonsense," as he called it, a rhapsodic verse whose only logic was that of feeling; and the heart, as against the head, was the battle cry of the *Sturm und Drang* generation, disciples, as they were, of Rousseau rather than Voltaire. Goethe was to adapt Voltaire for the German stage, coming out on the side of classicism and against one-sided nonsense or half-nonsense of any kind. Hence his opposition to the Romantic movement; but Nature and Art— noble savagery and civilization—remained the two poles of his unflagging poetic energy. Hölderlin's efforts to balance the two principles—to the point of trying to fuse Dionysus with Christ, of positing a "God of gods" so as to reconcile pantheism and polytheism with monotheism—broke him halfway through his life. Goethe's *Prometheus* is an example in this book of his dithyrambic manner. In a related poem, his *Wandrers Sturmlied,* he also resorted to a sublogical or superlogical syntax that came into its own, almost a century and a half later, in German Expressionism; and Hölderlin's late free verse, with its purely poetic or "architectonic" syntax, also became effective at the same time, just before the First World War.

The initiators of German Romanticism—represented here by the remarkable *Hymns to Night* of Novalis—did not break completely with these classical and classicizing antecedents, though it was Novalis who pioneered a portentous shift of concern away from classical antiquity to the Middle Ages. His *Hymns to Night* are partly in the rhymed forms that derive from the first of my "influences," Christian devotional verse, but partly in free verse or prose poetry—a medium whose cultivation by French poets did not begin until some three decades later. This rhythmic freedom has something to do with that introduced into German verse by the imitators of classical prosody, not excluding the misunderstood prosody of Pindar. Later Romantics were much more open to the third of my "influences," and it is this that dominates most of German nineteenth-century verse before Nietzsche.

It is the influence of folksong and popular ballads. A first wave of this influence, going back to Percy's *Reliques* but associated in Germany with the work of J. G. Herder, became pervasive in the 1770s, and gave rise to Goethe's songs and ballads of that period, as to Bürger's ballad *Lenore* of 1774. In their "classical" phase, Goethe and Schiller wrote ballads more didactic, elevated, and humanistic than demotic. A third wave followed with the publication of Brentano's and von Arnim's collection of folksongs *Des Knaben Wunderhorn* in 1808. Whereas Herder had collected folksongs of all nations, the Romantic cult of folk poetry tended more and more to be an expression of politically frustrated German nationalism, especially during the Napoleonic wars, when German states were repeatedly divided against one another, if not chopped up or dissolved. This return to popular modes had antecedents and counterparts in English literature, of course, even before the *Lyrical Ballads* of Wordsworth and Coleridge; but not to the extent of making songs and ballads as predominant as they became in German poetry almost throughout the nineteenth century.

A British scholar, E. M. Butler, wrote a book called *The Tyranny of Greece over Germany;* but, powerful though the impact of antiquity was on eighteenth-century Germany, as I have indicated, a still better case could be made for the tyranny of popular, or would-be popular, song and ballad over German poetry in the Romantic period. The musical connection must be relevant here. Goethe's lyrics were set to music repeatedly throughout the period covered by this anthology, by composers ranging in time and manner from Mozart to Hugo Wolf. From Beethoven to Brahms and Mahler, true, music also had a use for texts that were neither songs nor ballads, and did not in themselves "aspire to the condition of music." Yet it was the German "Lied," above all, that flourished throughout the century, both as a poetic and a musical genre.

The lyrics of Eichendorff are the purest instance of this aspiration to "the condition of music." Brentano's poems may have come still closer at times both to the spontaneity of folksong and sheer word music, but they were more idiosyncratic and less inviting to the composers. Heine, on the other hand, did appeal to the composers, though—as his prose works show—he was far too sophisticated, sceptical, and politically conscious a writer to feel comfortable within the Romantic conventions to which he half-conformed in most of his earlier and most popular lyrics. The characteristic sting in their tails, which could be self-destructive, enacts his dividedness and his unease. Heine's love for the old Germany of fairy tale and legend, of dreamers and metaphysicians, did not blind him to the escapist, anachronistic tendencies of Romantic art; and he was presciently aware of the political dangers inherent in German Romantic attitudes, which he satirized in his mock-epics and attacked in his prose.

Yet it was Mörike and Annette von Droste-Hülshoff who succeeded better than Heine in overcoming the limitations of Romantic song and ballad. Both these poets, for one thing, used their eyes and all their senses in a way that had become rare in German poetry, with its growing imperviousness to specific detail, to observed and lived realities, its harping on a generalized "nature" and the states of mind or heart projected into it. The sensuousness of Droste-Hülshoff's response to her immediate surroundings, her intense aliveness to their minutest phenomena, broke the tyranny of a would-be popular mode that had grown sentimental—a poetry of stock responses to obsolete folksy simplicities. Mörike, too, was as musical a poet as any of his predecessors; but, regional and traditionalist though he was, he brought a delicacy of perception and modulation to the pure lyric that infused new life into it.

Other poets again—from Platen and Rückert to C. F. Meyer—

tended toward an austere craftsmanship that made for firm out-
lines, rather than for that vagueness which Baudelaire saw as es-
sential to Romantic art. Toward the end of the century, it was so-
cially realistic preoccupations that impinged on the confessional,
backward-looking stereotype, as in Fontane's ballad on the Tay
Bridge disaster, or Ferdinand von Saar's poems about the labor-
ing poor and the new industrial scene (not included here). Like Keller
and Meyer, two outstanding Swiss writers, Fontane and von Saar
were primarily writers of prose fiction, and not of fairy tales, the
paradigm of German Romantic prose.

So much for the main trends, as I see them. Readers more sym-
pathetic than I am to the Romantic school and its protracted dom-
inance may see them differently, and I am aware that my survey is
not only partisan but cursory and full of gaps. It is readers, too,
who must fill those gaps by their attention not to trends, but to
poems I had no space even to mention.

It remains to be said that this is a bilingual anthology. As such,
it raises questions not only of selection, as raised by every anthology, but of translation and translatability. As regards the selection, I welcomed the work by so-called "minor" poets, beginning
with Salis-Seewis, because it is the function of anthologies to do
justice to poems, rather than to the status, major or minor, ac-
corded to their authors by the prevalent consensus. In fact it is certain "major" poets, like Goethe and Hölderlin here, who lend
themselves least to anthologization intended to be representative.
Goethe's poetry alone is so rich and various that no anthology on
this scale could possibly represent it; and within one decade—as
against Goethe's six and a half decades of work—Hölderlin
underwent a development so intense that it took another century
for his successors to catch up with it.

As for translatability, the editor of this anthology was wise enough
not to exclude old translations, like those by Coleridge, Longfellow, or the excellent and less familiar ones by the Irish poet Mangan, whose version of Bürger's long ballad could never have been
matched by a translator of our time. The translatability of a poem
does not depend on its degree of "difficulty." Some of the most
"difficult," complex, or even obscure poems are more translatable
than the "simplest" of lyrics, whose effectiveness may depend on
a concordance of sound with sense that cannot be reproduced in

another language. Some of Goethe's seemingly transparent lyrics and most of Eichendorff's are of that kind. Secondly, poems that are translatable in one age may be untranslatable in another, because faithful translation—by which I don't mean literal translation—calls for a degree of empathy and identification with their text that can become impossible for historical reasons, where attitudes, sensibilities, or diction are too far apart. Inevitably, therefore, representativeness and translatability will be at odds in an anthology covering so much ground. Coleridge, Mangan, and Longfellow had the advantage of being closer in attitude, sensibility, and diction to their particular texts. Perhaps I should confess that all but three of the poets in this anthology have proved untranslatable by me, if only because I felt no need to translate them. That makes me all the more appreciative of the many good translations to be found in this anthology, and less inclined to quibble with those that strike me as less good. One discovery, for me, was the translations, and translatability, of poems by Annette von Droste-Hülshoff. If an anthology can spring surprises of that sort—and it must hold different ones for other readers—it has done what an anthology can do.

MICHAEL HAMBURGER

Introduction

All compilers of anthologies place themselves in jeopardy, compilers of bilingual ones in double jeopardy, and if the translations in the latter be by many hands the risk is increased manyfold. So too, to be sure, is the chance of occasional success. And so the risk must be taken, for even occasional success in such instances is eminently rewarding, and against Robert Frost's discouraging, not to say smug, dictum that "poetry is what gets lost in translation" we can place Goethe's high-spirited words that "every translator is a prophet to his people." If there is a Frost, there is also a Pound, and a Dryden, Pope, Luther, Goethe, Shelley, a Nims, Leishman, Spender, and many, many more, none of whom heeded the council of despair. As George Steiner has said, "Arguments against verse translation are arguments against all translation," for there cannot be, even in prose, an "exhaustive transfer from language A to language B." No one knows this better than the translator himself and the more conscientious he is and the more thoroughly he understands the nature of poetry the more keenly will he be aware of it.

My present task was to compile within strict spatial limits as representative a selection as possible of German verse in English translation from Matthias Claudius (b. 1740) to Friedrich Nietzsche (d. 1900), a period that includes, at least for the student of German literature, perhaps two-thirds of the superlative poets of the German language, poets who were the contemporaries of the great German composers who followed in the wake of Bach as they themselves in the wake of Klopstock.

The composers, however, are universally known because of their

xxi · *Introduction*

universal language, while the poets whose names awaken some
gleam of recognition in the eyes of the Anglophone can almost be
counted on the fingers of one hand: Goethe, Schiller, Hölderlin,
Novalis, Heine, and Nietzsche (though hardly as a lyric poet). Who
has heard even of Mörike, a poet of the caliber of Keats? of Droste-
Hülshoff? of Brentano? of C. F. Meyer? of Lenau? Storm (as a
lyricist)? of Hölty, Claudius, Hebbel, yes, even of Eichendorff? In
our grandparents' and greatgrandparents' day a certain kind of
German verse was apparently better known. That of Uhland, for
example, and Anastasius Grün, Justinus Kerner, Karl Simrock,
Emanuel Geibel, Ferdinand Freiligrath. Most of these we now
consider deservedly forgotten. But it is not wise to be too self-as-
sured about our own taste. I have before me the fourth edition of
Theodor Storm's once popular *Hausbuch aus den deutschen Dich-
tern seit Claudius* (1878), and though Storm himself is in the
judgment of many (including Thomas Mann) one of the most perfect lyricists of the nineteenth century, his anthology teems with
names forgotten even to the specialist.

A word about the weighting of the poets represented here.
Hölderlin is of course grossly underrepresented. That is not due to
a lack of excellent translations of his work but to the fact that a
separate Hölderlin volume is scheduled to appear in The German
Library. The same is true for Heine (see volume 32 of this series)
and of course for Goethe. Weighting naturally also depends in part
upon the availability of acceptable translations. Everyone, it would
seem, has translated Heine. Many have "done" Goethe. Schiller is
available especially in nineteenth-century translations. Novalis's
Hymns to Night have been rendered into English at least four times
with varying success, the translation included here being the fourth.
Mörike has more recently received serious consideration at the hands
of Christopher Middleton and G. H. Chase and in this volume also
meticulous attention from J. B. Dallett. But a goodly number of
others—Brentano, Droste-Hülshoff, Hölty, Hebbel, Storm, for instance—have hardly received serious treatment from translators.

An anthologist of verse in translation who wishes to be representative must sometimes content himself with translations (including his own!) which he may consider somewhat less than completely successful. Nonetheless, when he can number among the
contributors to his venture such names as Hamburger, Middleton,

Nims, Lewisohn, Schoolfield, Salinger, Gode, not to speak of such classics as Mangan and Longfellow, he perhaps has no reason to complain. I am particularly grateful to those who were willing— at what expense of time, agonies of conscience, thumbing of rhyming dictionaries—to undertake special renderings for this collection. May it at least fill a gap for the time being and contribute in some measure to the life of the spirit, even though it may not always afford the elation Keats felt upon first looking into Chapman's Homer.

R.M.B.

Apart from the selections in this volume, additional poems of the period will be represented in other volumes of The German Library: J. W. v. Goethe in volume 20; F. Hölderlin in volume 22; H. Heine in volume 32. German poetry before M. Claudius may be found in volume 9, *German Poetry from the Beginnings to 1750;* poetry after F. Nietzsche in volume 69, *German Poetry of the Twentieth Century;* and in the volumes on R. M. Rilke (70), G. Benn (73), and B. Brecht (77). There will also be a volume on German texts that have been set to music, from folksongs to settings by composers like Bach, Beethoven, Schumann, and H. Wolf, in volume 85, *The German Lied.*

V.S.

German Poetry
from 1750 to 1900

Matthias Claudius

Der Säemann säet den Samen

Der Säemann säet den Samen,
  Die Erd empfängt ihn, und über ein kleines
  Keimet die Blume herauf—

Du liebtest sie. Was auch dies Leben
  Sonst für Gewinn hat, war klein dir geachtet,
  Und sie entschlummerte dir!

Was weinest du neben dem Grabe,
  Und hebst die Hände zur Wolke des Todes
  Und der Verwesung empor?

Wie Gras auf dem Felde sind Menschen
  Dahin, wie Blätter! Nur wenige Tage
  Gehn wir verkleidet einher!

Der Adler besuchet die Erde,
  Doch säumt nicht, schüttelt vom Flügel den Staub und
  Kehret zur Sonne zurück!

Abendlied

Der Mond ist aufgegangen,
Die goldnen Sternlein prangen
  Am Himmel hell und klar;
Der Wald steht schwarz und schweiget,
Und aus den Wiesen steiget
  Der weiße Nebel wunderbar.

Matthias Claudius

The sower is sowing his seed

The sower is sowing his seed and
   the earth receives it; and then in a trice the
      flowers are coming to bloom.

You did love her. This life, whatever
   blessings it offered, seemed otherwise trivial.
      And then she slumbered away!

Why weep now over the gravestone?
   Why raise your hands to the clouds, invoking
      Spectres of death and decay?

Like grass on the meadow we pass on,
   are swept like leaves! Oh so briefly we linger,
      costumed, then leave the world's stage.

The eagle pays earth a short visit,
   but tarries not—soon shakes the dust from his wings and
      then to the sun he returns.

Kenneth Negus

Evening Song

   The silver moon has risen.
   The starry heavens glisten
      In golden splendor clear.
   The woods stand mute and dreary,
   And from the pastures weary
      White fogs surge up afar and near.

Wie ist die Welt so stille
Und in der Dämmrung Hülle
   So traulich und so hold!
Als eine stille Kammer,
Wo ihr des Tages Jammer
   Verschlafen und vergessen sollt.

Seht ihr den Mond dort stehen?
Er ist nur halb zu sehen
   Und ist doch rund und schön!
So sind wohl manche Sachen,
Die wir getrost belachen,
   Weil unsre Augen sie nicht sehn.

Wir stolzen Menschenkinder
Sind eitel arme Sünder
   Und wissen gar nicht viel;
Wir spinnen Luftgespinste
Und suchen viele Künste
   Und kommen weiter von dem Ziel.

Gott, laß dein Heil uns schauen,
Auf nichts Vergänglichs trauen,
   Nicht Eitelkeit uns freun!
Laß uns einfältig werden
Und vor dir hier auf Erden
   Wie Kinder fromm und fröhlich sein!

Wollst endlich sonder Grämen
Aus dieser Welt uns nehmen
   Durch einen sanften Tod!
Und wenn du uns genommen,
Laß uns in Himmel kommen,
   Du, unser Herr und unser Gott!

So legt euch denn, ihr Brüder,
In Gottes Namen nieder!
   Kalt ist der Abendhauch.

The world looks calm and rested,
In twilight shadows vested
  So friendly and so warm.
Just like a quiet shelter
Where you forget the welter
  Of life's distress and every storm.

The moon seems to be growing,
With half of it just showing,
  Yet it is round and fair.
'Tis once again a matter
Of which we blithely chatter
  Though it is not for us to bare.

Prideful, yet mere beginners,
Poor souls we are and sinners,
  We error-stricken souls.
We dream of building towers,
Seek ever greater powers
  And yet stray farther from our goal.

Lord, let us see salvation,
Distrust our passing station
  And earthly revelry.
Teach us the joys of meekness,
Of strength—beyond man's weakness—
  In childlike trust and piety.

And when the time is ready,
Grant that, serene and steady,
  We heed death's gentle nod.
And let us—simple mortals—
Pass through the pearly portals,
  You, our Lord and our God.

Go, brethren, to—God willing—
Your daily round fulfilling,
  To rest, each in his room.

Verschon uns, Gott, mit Strafen
Und laß uns ruhig schlafen
   Und unsern kranken Nachbar auch!

Die Sternseherin Lise

Ich sehe oft um Mitternacht,
Wenn ich mein Werk getan
Und niemand mehr im Hause wacht,
Die Stern am Himmel an.

Sie gehn da, hin und her zerstreut,
Als Lämmer auf der Flur,
In Rudeln auch und aufgereiht
Wie Perlen an der Schnur.

Und funkeln alle weit und breit
Und funkeln rein und schön;
Ich seh die große Herrlichkeit
Und kann mich satt nicht sehn . . .

Dann saget unterm Himmelszelt
Mein Herz mir in der Brust:
„Es gibt was Bessers in der Welt
Als all ihr Schmerz und Lust.‟

Ich werf mich auf mein Lager hin
Und liege lange wach
Und suche es in meinem Sinn;
Und sehne mich darnach.

Save us, God, from disaster,
Bless our sleep, O Master,
 And our ailing neighbor's, too.

Alexander Gode

The Stargazing Maiden

At midnight, after everyone
Has gone to sleep, then I
So often, when my work is done,
Gaze at the stars on high.

They move at random to and fro
Like young lambs pasturing;
They pass in flocks or in a row,
Like pearls strung on a string.

And far and wide all twinkle bright
And twinkle pure and still.
I see the splendor of that sight
And cannot get my fill.

Then under heaven's vault my heart
Within me tells me plain,
"The world has something to impart
Beyond its joy and pain."

I throw myself upon my bed
And long I toss and turn,
And ponder what my heart has said,
And lie awake and yearn.

Sheema Z. Buehne

Kriegslied

's ist Krieg! 's ist Krieg! O Gottes Engel wehre
Und rede Du darein!
's ist leider Krieg—und ich begehre
Nicht schuld daran zu sein!

Was sollt ich machen, wenn im Schlaf mit Grämen
Und blutig, bleich und blaß
Die Geister der Erschlagnen zu mir kämen
Und vor mir weinten, was?

Wenn wackre Männer, die sich Ehre suchten,
Verstümmelt und halb tot
Im Staub sich vor mir wälzten und mir fluchten
In ihrer Todesnot?

Wenn tausend, tausend Väter, Mütter, Bräute,
So glücklich vor dem Krieg,
Nun alle elend, alle arme Leute,
Wehklagten über mich?

Wenn Hunger, böse Seuch und ihre Nöten
Freund, Freund und Feind ins Grab
Versammleten, und mir zu Ehren krähten
Von einer Leich herab?

Was hülf mir Kron und Land und Gold und Ehre?
Die könnten mich nicht freun!
s'ist leider Krieg—und ich begehre
Nicht schuld daran zu sein!

A Song of War

The world's at war! O powers above, conspire
To quench the hideous flame!
Alas the war! And I may but desire
That mine be not the blame.

What should I do, if in my dreams the slaughtered
Pale rising should appear,
Bloody accusing ghosts, and silent watered
My bed with many a tear?

If good men, whom my cruel will coerces,
Maimed, wounded unto death,
Should writhe before me in the mire, with curses
Upon their dying breath?

If all these thousands, children, fathers, mothers,
Once happy, sheltered, fed,
Now wretched all, poor people, for those others
Cried woe upon my head?

If want and horror, pestilence, starvation,
Once their dread work were done,
Should gather friend and foe in execration
Of me, the guilty one?

What worth all power to which I might aspire,
The glory and acclaim?
Alas the war! And I may but desire
That mine be not the blame.

Albert Bloch

Christiane

Es stand ein Sternlein am Himmel,
   Ein Sternlein guter Art;
Das tät so lieblich scheinen,
   So lieblich und so zart!

Ich wußte seine Stelle
   Am Himmel, wo es stand;
Trat abends vor die Schwelle,
   Und suchte, bis ich's fand;

Und blieb denn lange stehen,
   Hatt große Freud in mir:
Das Sternlein anzusehen;
   Und dankte Gott dafür.

Das Sternlein ist verschwunden;
   Ich suche hin und her
Wo ich es sonst gefunden,
   Und find es nun nicht mehr.

Der Tod und das Mädchen

Das Mädchen

Vorüber! Ach, vorüber!
Geh wilder Knochenmann!
Ich bin noch jung, geh Lieber!
Und rühre mich nicht an.

Telescope

Christiane

A star stood in the heavens,
a little, charming light,
that always shone so sweetly,
so softly through the night.

I knew the stars around it
and where its place should lie
and sought until I found it
in every evening sky.

I used to watch it yonder,
so dainty and so far,
and, filled with joy and wonder,
I thanked God for the star.

The star has vanished, vainly
I seek it from my door,
but where I saw it plainly,
I find it now no more.

J. W. Thomas

Death and the Girl

Girl:

Pass by! O pass me by!
Away, wild mask of death!
I still am young! O why
destroy me with your breath?

Der Tod

Gib deine Hand, du schön und zart Gebild!
Bin Freund, und komme nicht, zu strafen.
Sei gutes Muts! ich bin nicht wild,
Sollst sanft in meinen Armen schlafen!

Der Tod

Ach, es ist so dunkel in des Todes Kammer,
   Tönt so traurig, wenn er sich bewegt
Und nun aufhebt seinen schweren Hammer
   Und die Stunde schlägt.

Gottfried August Bürger

Lenore

   Lenore fuhr ums Morgenrot
Empor aus schweren Träumen:
„Bist untreu, Wilhelm, oder tot?
Wie lange willst du säumen?"—
Er war mit König Friedrichs Macht
Gezogen in die Prager Schlacht
Und hatte nicht geschrieben,
Ob er gesund geblieben.

Death:

Give me your hand, you lovely, tender child;
I am your friend and bring no harm.
Have courage. See, I am not wild;
now go to sleep upon my arm.

J. W. Thomas

Death

O the darkness of Death's chamber,
ounds so dismal when he starts his rounds,
?n uplifts his heavy, fateful hammer
And the hour resounds.

R. M. Browning

Gottfried August Bürger

Leonore

A Ballad

Upstarting with the dawning red,
    Rose Leonore from dreams of ill.
"Oh, Wilhelm! art thou false, or dead?
    How long, how long, wilt loiter still?"—
The youth had gone to Prague to yield
King Frederick aid in battle-field,
Nor word nor friend had come to tell
If he were still alive and well.

Der König und die Kaiserin,
Des langen Haders müde,
Erweichten ihren harten Sinn
Und machten endlich Friede;
Und jedes Heer, mit Sing und Sang,
Mit Paukenschlag und Kling und Klang,
Geschmückt mit grünen Reisern,
Zog heim zu seinen Häusern.

Und überall, allüberall,
Auf Wegen und auf Stegen,
Zog alt und jung dem Jubelschall
Der Kommenden entgegen.
Gottlob! rief Kind und Gattin laut,
Willkommen! manche frohe Braut.
Ach! aber für Lenoren
War Gruß und Kuß verloren.

Sie frug den Zug wohl auf und ab,
Und frug nach allen Namen;
Doch keiner war, der Kundschaft gab,
Von allen, so da kamen.
Als nun das Heer vorüber war,
Zerraufte sie ihr Rabenhaar,
Und warf sich hin zur Erde,
Mit wütiger Gebärde.

Die Mutter lief wohl hin zu ihr:
„Ach, daß sich Gott erbarme!
Du trautes Kind, was ist mit dir?"
Und schloß sie in die Arme.—
„O Mutter, Mutter! hin ist hin!
Nun fahre Welt und alles hin!
Bei Gott ist kein Erbarmen.
O weh, o weh mir Armen!"—

„Hilf Gott, hilf! Sieh uns gnädig an!
Kind, bet ein Vaterunser!
Was Gott tut, das ist wohlgetan.

War's trumpet blew its dying blast,
   And o'er the empress and the king
Long-wished, long looked-for Peace at last
   Came hovering upon angel-wing.
And all the hosts, with glittering sheen,
And kettledrum and tambourine,
And decked with garlands green and gay,
Marched, merrily, for home away.

And on the highways, paths, and byways,
   Came clustering, mustering, crowds and groups
Of old and young, from far and nigh-ways,
   And met with smiles the noble troops.
"Thank GOD!" the son and mother cried—
And "Welcome!" many a joyous bride:
But none throughout that happy meeting
Hailed Leonore with kiss or greeting.

She wandered hither, hurried thither;
   She called aloud upon her Lost,
But none knew aught of him she sought,
   Of all that far-extending host.
When all was vain, for sheer despair
She madly tore her night-black hair,
And dashed herself against the stones,
And raved and wept with bitter groans.

Then came her mother hurriedly—
   "Oh, GOD of Mercy!—what alarms
My darling child? What troubles thee?"—
   And locked her fondly in her arms.
"Oh, mother, mother! dead is dead!
My days are sped, my hopes are fled:
Heaven has no pity on me—none—
Oh, woe is me! oh, wretched one!"

"Alas! alas! Child, place thy trust
   In GOD, and raise thy heart above:
What GOD ordains is right and just,

Gott, Gott erbarmt sich unser!"—
„O Mutter, Mutter! Eitler Wahn!
Gott hat an mir nicht wohlgetan!
Was half, was half mein Beten?
Nun ist's nicht mehr vonnöten."—

„Hilf Gott, hilf! wer den Vater kennt,
Der weiß, er hilft den Kindern.
Das hochgelobte Sakrament
Wird deinen Jammer lindern."—
„O Mutter, Mutter! was mich brennt,
Das lindert mir kein Sakrament!
Kein Sakrament mag Leben
Den Toten wiedergeben."—

„Hör, Kind! wie, wenn der falsche Mann,
Im fernen Ungerlande,
Sich seines Glaubens abgetan,
Zum neuen Ehebande?
Laß fahren, Kind, sein Herz dahin!
Er hat es nimmermehr Gewinn!
Wann Seel und Leib sich trennen,
Wird ihn sein Meineid brennen."—

„O Mutter, Mutter! Hin ist hin!
Verloren ist verloren!
Der Tod, der Tod ist mein Gewinn!
O wär ich nie geboren!
Lisch aus, mein Licht, auf ewig aus!
Stirb hin, stirb hin in Nacht und Graus!
Bei Gott ist kein Erbarmen.
O weh, o weh mir Armen!"—

„Hilf Gott, hilf! Geh nicht ins Gericht
Mit deinem armen Kinde!
Sie weiß nicht, was die Zunge spricht.
Behalt ihr nicht die Sünde!
Ach, Kind, vergiß dein irdisch Leid,
Und denk an Gott und Seligkeit!

He is a GOD of tender love."—
"Oh! mother, mother! false and vain,
For GOD has wrought me only pain!
I will not pray—my plaint and prayer
Are wasted on the idle air!"

"No, no, my child!—not so—the LORD
   Is good—He heals His children's grief;
The Holy Eucharist will afford
   The anguish of thy soul relief."—
"Hush, mother, mother! What I feel
No Eucharist can ever heal—
No Eucharist can ever give
The shrouded Dead again to live."

"Ah, child, perchance thy lover now—
   A traitor to his love and thee—
Before the altar plights his vow
   To some fair girl of Hungary:
Yet weep not this perfidious wrong,
For he will rue it late and long,
And when his soul and body part
His faithlessness will burn his heart."

"Oh, mother, mother! gone is gone,
   And lorn for once is ever lorn!
The grave is now my hope alone:
   Would GOD that I had ne'er been born!
Out, out, sick light! Out, flickering taper!
Down, down in night and charnel vapour!
In Heaven there is no pity—none—
Oh, woe is me! oh, wretched one!"

"Oh, GOD of mercy, enter not
   In judgment with thy suffering child!
Condemn her not—she knows not what
   She raves in this delirium wild.
My child, forget thy tears and sighs,
And look to GOD and Paradise:

So wird doch deiner Seelen
Der Bräutigam nicht fehlen."—

„O Mutter! Was ist Seligkeit?
O Mutter! Was ist Hölle?
Bei ihm, bei ihm ist Seligkeit,
Und ohne Wilhelm Hölle!—
Lisch aus, mein Licht, auf ewig aus!
Stirb hin, stirb hin in Nacht und Graus!
Ohn ihn mag ich auf Erden,
Mag dort nicht selig werden."———

So wütete Verzweifelung
Ihr in Gehirn und Adern.
Sie fuhr mit Gottes Vorsehung
Vermessen fort zu hadern;
Zerschlug den Busen, und zerrang
Die Hand, bis Sonnenuntergang,
Bis auf am Himmelsbogen
Die goldnen Sterne zogen.

Und außen, horch! ging's trap trap trap,
Als wie von Rosseshufen;
Und klirrend stieg ein Reiter ab,
An des Geländers Stufen;
Und horch! und horch! den Pfortenring
Ganz lose, leise, klinglingling!
Dann kamen durch die Pforte
Vernehmlich diese Worte:

„Holla, Holla! Tu auf mein Kind!
Schläfst, Liebchen, oder wachst du?
Wie bist noch gegen mich gesinnt?
Und weinest oder lachst du?"—
„Ach, Wilhelm, du?—So spät bei Nacht?—
Geweinet hab ich und gewacht;
Ach, großes Leid erlitten!
Wo kommst du hergeritten?"—

A holier bridegroom shalt thou see,
And He will sweetly comfort thee."

"Oh, mother, what is Paradise?
  Oh, mother, what and where is Hell?
In Wilhelm lies my Paradise—
  Where he is not my life is Hell!
Then out, sick light! Out, flickering taper
Down, down in blackest night and vapour!
In heaven, on earth I will not share
Delight if Wilhelm be not there!"

And thus, as reigned and raged despair
  Throughout her brain, through every vein,
Did this presumptuous maiden dare
  To tax with ill GOD's righteous will,
And wrang her hands and beat her breast
Till sank the sunlight in the west,
And under heaven's ethereal arch
The silver stars began their march.

When, list! a sound!—hark! *hoff, hoff, hoff!*
  It nears, she hears a courser's tramp—
And swiftly bounds a rider off
  Before the gate with clattering stamp;
And hark, the bell goes *ring, ding, ding!*
And hark again! *cling, ling, ling, ling!*
And through the portal and the hall
There peals a voice with hollow call:

"What, ho! Up, up, sweet love inside!
  Dost watch for me, or art thou sleeping?
Art false, or still my faithful bride?
  And smilest thou, or art thou weeping?"—
"What! Wilhelm! thou? and come thus late!
Oh! Night has seen me weep and wait
And suffer so! But oh! I fear—
Why this wild haste in riding here?"

„Wir satteln nur um Mitternacht.
Weit ritt ich her von Böhmen.
Ich habe spät mich aufgemacht,
Und will dich mit mir nehmen."—
„Ach, Wilhelm, erst herein geschwind!
Den Hagedorn durchsaust der Wind,
Herein, in meinen Armen,
Herzliebster, zu erwarmen!"—

„Laß sausen durch den Hagedorn,
Laß sausen, Kind, laß sausen!
Der Rappe scharrt; es klirrt der Sporn.
Ich darf allhier nicht hausen.
Komm, schürze, spring' und schwinge dich
Auf meinen Rappen hinter mich!
Muß heut noch hundert Meilen
Mit dir ins Brautbett eilen."—

„Ach! wolltest hundert Meilen noch
Mich heut ins Braubett tragen?
Und horch! es brummt die Glocke noch,
Die elf schon angeschlagen."—
„Sieh hin, sieh her! der Mond scheint hell.
Wir und die Toten reiten schnell.
Ich bringe dich, zur Wette,
Noch heut ins Hochzeitsbette."—

„Sag an, wo ist dein Kämmerlein?
Wo? Wie dein Hochzeitsbettchen?"—
„Weit, weit von hier!—Still, kühl und klein!—
Sechs Bretter und zwei Brettchen!"—
„Hat's Raum für mich?"—„Für dich und mich!
Komm, schürze, spring und schwinge dich!
Die Hochzeitsgäste hoffen;
Die Kammer steht uns offen."—

Schön Liebchen schürzte, sprang und schwang
Sich auf das Roß behende;
Wohl um den trauten Reiter schlang

"I left Bohemia late at night:
   We journey but at midnight, we!
My time was brief, and fleet my flight.
   Up, up! thou must away with me!"—
"Ah, Wilhelm! come inside the house;
The wind moans through the firtree boughs;
Come in, my heart's beloved! and rest
And warm thee in this faithful breast."

"The boughs may wave, the wind may rave;
   Let rave the blast and wave the fir!
Though winds may rave and boughs may wave
   My sable steed expects the spur.
Up! gird thyself, and spring with speed
Behind me on my sable steed!
A hundred leagues must yet be sped
Before we reach the bridal bed."

"Oh, Wilhelm! at so drear an hour,
   A hundred leagues away from bed!
Hark! hark! 'Eleven' from the tower
   Is tolling far with tone of dread!"
"Look round! look up! The moon is bright.
The Dead and We are fleet of flight:
Doubt not I'll bear thee hence away
To home before the break of day."

"And where is then the nuptial hall?
   And where the chamber of the bride?"
"Far, far from hence! Chill, still, and small,
   But six feet long by two feet wide!"
"Hast room for me?" "For me and thee!
Quick! robe thyself and come with me.
The wedding guests await the bride;
The chamber-door stands open wide."

Soon up, soon clad, with lightest bound
   On that black steed the maiden sprung,
And round her love, and warmly round,

Sie ihre Lilienhände!
Und hurre hurre, hop hop hop!
Ging's fort in sausendem Galopp,
Daß Roß und Reiter schnoben,
Und Kies und Funken stoben.

    Zur rechten und zur linken Hand,
Vorbei vor ihren Blicken,
Wie flogen Anger, Heid und Land!
Wie donnerten die Brücken!—
„Graut Liebchen auch?—Der Mond scheint hell!
Hurra! die Toten reiten schnell!
Graut Liebchen auch vor Toten?"—
„Ach nein!—Doch laß die Toten!"—

    Was klang dort für Gesang und Klang?
Was flatterten die Raben?—
Horch Glockenklang! horch Totensang:
„Laßt uns den Leib begraben!"
Und näher zog ein Leichenzug,
Der Sarg und Totenbahre trug.
Das Lied war zu vergleichen
Dem Unkenruf in Teichen.

    „Nach Mitternacht begrabt den Leib,
Mit Klang und Sang und Klage!
Jetzt führ ich heim mein junges Weib,
Mit, mit zum Brautgelage!
Komm, Küster, hier! Komm mit dem Chor,
Und gurgle mit das Brautlied vor!
Komm, Pfaff, und sprich den Segen,
Eh wir zu Bett uns legen!"—

    Still Klang und Sang.—Die Bahre schwand.—
Gehorsam seinem Rufen,
Kam's, hurre hurre! nachgerannt,
Hart hinter's Rappen Hufen.
Und immer weiter, hop hop hop!
Ging's fort in sausendem Galopp,

Her snow-white arms she swung and flung;
And deftly, swiftly, *hoff, hoff, hoff!*
Away went horse and riders off;
Till panted horse and riders too,
And sparks and pebbles flashed and flew!

On left and right, with whirling flight,
   How rock and forest reeled and wheeled!
How danced each height before their sight!
   What thunder-tones the bridges pealed!
"Dost fear! The moon is fair to see;
Hurrah! the Dead ride rapidly!
Beloved! dost dread the shrouded Dead?"
"Ah, no! but let them rest," she said.

But see! what throng, with song and gong
   Moves by, as croaks the raven hoarse!
Hark! funeral song! Hark! knelling dong!
   They sing, "Let's here inter the corpse!"
And nearer draws that mourning throng,
And bearing hearse and bier along.
With hollow hymn outgurgled like
Low reptile groanings from a dyke.

"Entomb your dead when midnight wanes,
   With knell, and bell, and funeral wail!
Now homewards to her dim domains
   I bear my bride—so, comrades, hail!
Come, Sexton, with the choral throng,
And jabber me the bridal song.
Come, Priest, the marriage must be blessed
Before the wedded pair can rest!"

Some spell is in the horseman's call,
   The hymn is hushed, the hearse is gone,
And in his wake the buriers all,
   Tramp, tramp, come clattering, pattering on;
And onward, forward, *hoff, hoff, hoff!*
Away swept all in gallop off,

Daß Roß und Reiter schnoben,
Und Kies und Funken stoben.

Wie flogen rechts, wie flogen links,
Gebirge, Bäum und Hecken!
Wie flogen links, und rechts, und links
Die Dörfer, Städt und Flecken!—
„Graut Liebchen auch? Der Mond scheint hell!
Hurra! die Toten reiten schnell!
Graut Liebchen auch vor Toten?"—
„Ach! Laß sie ruhn die Toten!"—

Sieh da! sieh da! Am Hochgericht
Tanzt, um des Rades Spindel
Halb sichtbarlich bei Mondenlicht,
Ein luftiges Gesindel.—
„Sasa! Gesindel, hier! Komm hier!
Gesindel, komm und folge mir!
Tanz uns den Hochzeitreigen,
Wann wir zu Bette steigen!"—

Und das Gesindel husch husch husch!
Kam hinten nachgeprasselt,
Wie Wirbelwind am Haselbusch
Durch dürre Blätter rasselt.
Und weiter, weiter, hop hop hop!
Ging's fort in sausendem Galopp,
Daß Roß und Reiter schnoben,
Und Kies und Funken stoben.

Wie flog, was rund der Mond beschien,
Wie flog es in die Ferne!
Wie flogen oben über hin
Der Himmel und die Sterne!—
„Graut Liebchen auch?—Der Mond scheint hell!
Hurra! Die Toten reiten schnell!
Graut Liebchen auch vor Toten?"—
„O weh! Laß ruhn die Toten!"———

Till panted steeds and riders too,
And sparks and pebbles flashed and flew.

On left and right, with flight of light,
  How whirled the hills, the trees, the bowers!
With lightlike flight, on left and right,
  How spun the hamlets, towns, and towers!
"Dost quail! The moon is fair to see;
Hurrah! the Dead ride recklessly!
Beloved! dost dread the shrouded Dead?"
"Ah! let the Dead repose!" she said.

But look! On yonder gibbet's height,
  How round his wheel, as wanly glances
The yellow moon's unclouded light,
  A malefactor's carcase dances!
"So ho! poor Carcase! down with thee!
Down, Thing of Bones, and follow me!
And thou shalt briskly dance, ho, ho!
Before us when to bed we go!"

Whereon the Carcase, *brush, ush, ush!*
  Came rustling, bustling, close behind,
With whirr as when through hazel-bush,
  Steals cracklingly the winter wind.
And forward, onward, *hoff, hoff, hoff!*
Away dashed all in gallop off,
Till panted steeds and riders too,
And fire and pebbles flashed and flew.

How swift the eye saw sweep and fly
  Earth's bounding car afar, afar!
How flew on high the circling sky,
  The heavens and every winking star.
"Dost quake? The moon is fair to see.
Hurrah! the Dead ride gloriously!
Beloved! dost dread the shrouded Dead?"
"Oh woe! let rest the Dead!" she said.

„Rapp! Rapp! Mich dünkt, der Hahn schon ruft.—
Bald wird der Sand verrinnen—
Rapp! Rapp! Ich wittre Morgenluft—
Rapp! Tummle dich von hinnen!—
Vollbracht, vollbracht ist unser Lauf!
Das Hochzeitbette tut sich auf!
Die Toten reiten schnelle!
Wir sind, wir sind zur Stelle."————

    Rasch auf ein eisern Gittertor
Ging's mit verhängtem Zügel.
Mit schwanker Gert ein Schlag davor
Zersprengte Schloß und Riegel.
Die Flügel flogen klirrend auf,
Und über Gräber ging der Lauf.
Es blinkten Leichensteine
Rund um im Mondenscheine.

    Ha sieh! Ha sieh! im Augenblick,
Huhu! ein gräßlich Wunder!
Des Reiters Koller, Stück für Stück,
Fiel ab, wie mürber Zunder.
Zum Schädel, ohne Zopf und Schopf,
Zum nackten Schädel ward sein Kopf;
Sein Körper zum Gerippe,
Mit Stundenglas und Hippe.

    Hoch bäumte sich, wild schnob der Rapp
Und sprühte Feuerfunken;
Und hui! war's unter ihr hinab
Verschwunden und versunken.
Geheul! Geheul aus hoher Luft,
Gewinsel kam aus tiefer Gruft.
Lenorens Herz, mit Beben,
Rang zwischen Tod und Leben.

    Nun tanzten wohl bei Mondenglanz,
Rund um herum im Kreise,
Die Geister einen Kettentanz,

" 'Tis well! Ha! ha! the cock is crowing;
    Thy sand, Beloved, is nearly run!
I smell the breeze of Morning blowing.
    My good black steed, thy race is done!
The race is done, the goal is won—
The wedding bed we shall not shun!
The Dead can chase and race apace!
Behold! we face the fated place!"

Before a grated portal stand
    That midnight troop and coalblack horse,
Which, touched as by a viewless wand,
    Bursts open with gigantic force!
With trailing reins and lagging speed
Wends onward now the gasping steed,
Where ghastily the moon illumes
A wilderness of graves and tombs!

He halts. O horrible! Behold—
    Hoo! hoo! behold a hideous wonder!
The rider's garments drop like mould
    Of crumbling plasterwork asunder!
His skull, in bony nakedness,
Glares hairless, fleshless, featureless!
And now a skeleton he stands,
With flashing Scythe and Glass of Sands!

High roars the barb—he snorts—be winks—
    His nostrils flame—his eyeballs glow—
And, whirl! the maiden sinks and sinks
    Down in the smothering clay below!
Then howls and shrieks in air were blended;
And wailings from the graves ascended,
Until her heart, in mortal strife,
Wrestled with very Death for Life!

And now, as dimmer moonlight wanes,
    Round Leonore in shadowy ring
The spectres dance their dance of chains,

Und heulten diese Weise:
„Geduld! Geduld! Wenn's Herz auch bricht!
Mit Gott im Himmel hadre nicht!
Des Leibes bist du ledig;
Gott sei der Seele gnädig!"

Ludwig Christoph Heinrich Hölty

Auftrag

Ihr Freunde hänget, wann ich gestorben bin,
Die kleine Harfe hinter dem Altar auf,
    Wo an der Wand die Totenkränze
      Manches verstorbenen Mädchens schimmern.

Der Küster zeigt dann freundlich dem Reisenden
Die kleine Harfe, rauscht mit dem roten Band,
    Das, an der Harfe festgeschlungen,
      Unter den goldenen Saiten flattert.

„Oft", sagt er staunend, „tönen im Abendrot
Von selbst die Saiten, leise wie Bienenton:
    Die Kinder, auf dem Kirchhof spielend,
      Hörten's und sahn, wie die Kränze bebten." *

---

* Last stanza added by Johann Heinrich Voss (1751–18﹖﹖

And howlingly she hears them sing—
"Bear, bear, although thy heart be riven!
And tamper not with GOD in heaven.
Thy body's knell they soon shall toll—
May GOD have mercy on thy soul!"

James Clarence Mangan

Ludwig Christoph Heinrich Hölty

Mandate

(Alcaics)

Oh friends, when I am dead, take the little lyre
And hang it behind the altar, at the place
Where on the wall the funeral garlands
Shimmer for many a death-fetched maiden.

The kindly sexton will show the little lyre
To the traveler then, and ruffle its band of red
Which, woven snug around the frame, will
Flutter beneath the golden harpstrings.

Amazed, he'll tell him: "Often, at eventide,
Untouched, the strings resound, soft as humming bees;
The children playing in the churchyard
Heard it and saw how the garlands trembled."

G. C. Schoolfield

Die Schale der Vergessenheit

Eine Schale des Stroms, welcher Vergessenheit
   Durch Elysiums Blumen rollt,
Eine Schale des Stroms spende mir, Genius!
   Dort wo Phaons die Sängerin,
Dort wo Orpheus vergaß seiner Eurydice,
   Schöpf die goldene Urne voll!
Dann versenk ich dein Bild, spröde Gebieterin,
   In den silbernen Schlummerquell!
Den allsiegenden Blick, der mir im Marke zuckt,
   Und das Beben der weißen Brust,
Und die süße Musik, welche der Lipp' entfloß,
   Tauch ich tief in den Schlummerquell!

An den Abendstern

Heil dir, Hesper! mit dem milden Antlitz! Blinkest
Du am rotgemalten Abendhimmel, winkest
Du dem Jüngling und dem Mädchen schon im Hain
Treuen Küssen sich zu weihn?

Küssen, die so lieblich durch die Dämmrung rauschen,
Daß die Waldgöttinnen wonnetrunken lauschen,
Nach dem Jüngling schielen, voller Lüsternheit,
Nach dem Mädchen voller Neid.

Wie die treuen wandeln, Arm in Arm geschlossen,
Durch die mondbeglänzten Schatten, ganz zerflossen
In Entzückung, die den Busen feurig hebt,
Und in jeder Ader bebt.

The Cup of Oblivion

(Second Asclepiadean Reversed)

But one cup from that stream, bearing oblivion
  Through Elysium's flowered fields,
But one cup from that stream grant me, oh guardian!
  There where Phaon fled Sappho's soul,
There where Orpheus lost thought of Eurydice—
  Fill this goblet of gold for me!
Then I shall sink your face, mistress who will not yield,
  In the silvery well of sleep,
That all-triumphant glance, shot to my very heart,
  Those white breasts in their quivering,
And that music which sweet flowed from your lips to me:
  All plunged into the well of sleep!

G. C. *Schoolfield*

To the Evening Star

Hail, Hesperus, whose gentle face is blinking
in the painted evening heavens! Are you winking
to the youth and maiden in the wood below,
saying, "Kiss before you go"?

Kisses murmur through the graying dusk so sweetly
that ecstatic forest goddesses discreetly
listen as they eye the youth with shameless lust
and the maiden with distrust.

So the lovers pass, embracing ever fonder,
through the moonlit shadows silently they wander.
With delight their breathing labors as with pain;
rapture burns in every vein.

Duftet süßer, wo sie wandeln, Frühlingsrosen,
Deren junge Busen Abendlüftchen kosen,
Lispelt, Bäche, die durch Blumentäler fliehn,
Angenehmre Melodien.

Gieße hellre Zaubereien aus der Kehle,
Kleiner süßer Vogel, liebe Philomele,
Lächle durch das Laubgewölbe, Hesperus,
Reizender, bei jedem Kuß.

Johann Wolfgang von Goethe

Mailied

Wie herrlich leuchtet
Mir die Natur!
Wie glänzt die Sonne!
Wie lacht die Flur!

Es dringen Blüten
Aus jedem Zweig
Und tausend Stimmen
Aus dem Gesträuch

Und Freud und Wonne
Aus jeder Brust.
O Erd, o Sonne!
O Glück, o Lust!

O Lieb, o Liebe!
So golden schön,
Wie Morgenwolken
Auf jenen Höhn!

Springtime roses, spread the fragrance of your dresses,
as the evening wind your youthful breasts caresses;
whisper, brooks, through darkened glades and trees
ever sweeter melodies.

Pour forth, nightingale, your fairest, brightest fancy,
all your magic spells and secret necromancy;
smile, O Hesperus, through vaults of leafy lace
temptingly with each embrace.

J. W. Thomas

Johann Wolfgang von Goethe

May Song

How fine a light on
Nature today!
The sun's in glory!
The fields at play!

What feats of blossom
A twig achieves!
A thousand voices
Delight the leaves!

And every pleasure
For girl, for boy!
The sun-warm country
Of joy on joy!

Oh love! O lovely!
My golden girl!
Like clouds at morning
Your rose and pearl!

Du segnest herrlich
Das frische Feld,
Im Blütendampfe
Die volle Welt.

O Mädchen, Mädchen,
Wie lieb ich dich!
Wie blickt dein Auge!
Wie liebst du mich!

So liebt die Lerche
Gesang und Luft,
Und Morgenblumen
Den Himmelsduft,

Wie ich dich liebe
Mit warmem Blut,
Die du mir Jugend
Und Freud und Mut

Zu neuen Liedern
Und Tänzen gibst.
Sei ewig glücklich,
Wie du mich liebst!

Willkommen und Abschied

Es schlug mein Herz, geschwind zu Pferde!
Es war getan fast eh gedacht.
Der Abend wiegte schon die Erde,
Und an den Bergen hing die Nacht;
Schon stand im Nebelkleid die Eiche,
Ein aufgetürmter Riese, da,
Wo Finsternis aus dem Gesträuche
Mit hundert schwarzen Augen sah.

You lean in blessing
On earth's cool bloom,
The world a richness of
Dense perfume!

O darling, darling!
I'm wild for you!
Your lashes dazzle:
You love me too!

The lark loves singing
Away up there;
The flowers at morning
Delight in the air,

As I adore you, with
Blood a-thrill!
It's youth you give me,
Ecstatic will

For newer music
And dancing! Be
In bliss forever,
As you love me!

John Frederick Nims

The Meeting, The Departure

My pulses rushed, and, quick, to saddle!
No sooner thought about than—done!
With evening easy in her cradle
And dark hills covering the sun.
In wraiths of vapor hooded, towering,
The oak tree—what a giant!—there.
In shrubs a hundred eyes were glowering,
The dark—observant everywhere.

Der Mond von einem Wolkenhügel
Sah kläglich aus dem Duft hervor,
Die Winde schwangen leise Flügel,
Umsausten schauerlich mein Ohr;
Die Nacht schuf tausend Ungeheuer,
Doch frisch und fröhlich war mein Mut:
In meinen Adern welches Feuer!
In meinem Herzen welche Glut!

Dich sah ich, und die milde Freude
Floß von dem süßen Blick auf mich;
Ganz war mein Herz an deiner Seite
Und jeder Atemzug für dich.
Ein rosenfarbnes Frühlingswetter
Umgab das liebliche Gesicht,
Und Zärtlichkeit für mich—ihr Götter!
Ich hofft es, ich verdient es nicht!

Doch ach, schon mit der Morgensonne
Verengt der Abschied mir das Herz:
In deinen Küssen welche Wonne!
In deinem Auge welcher Schmerz!
Ich ging, du standst und sahst zur Erden,
Und sahst mir nach mit nassem Blick:
Und doch, welch Glück, geliebt zu werden!
Und lieben, Götter, welch ein Glück!

Im Herbst 1775

Fetter grüne, du Laub,
Das Rebengeländer,
Hier mein Fenster herauf.
Gedrängter quillet,
Zwillingsbeeren, und reifet

The moon already peaked with grieving
Through cloudy cover leaned to peer.
The nightwind stirred its feathers, leaving
A wail and shudder at my ear.
The darkness crawled with *things,* surrounding
The cruppers—I was buoyant though!
What ardor in the blood abounding!
Along the pulses what a glow!

I saw you, in your eye the greeting
That floods me—sweetness through and through.
For you alone my heart was beating;
For you alone the breath I drew.
Your face a glory: May and roses
Its native weather! Such concern
For me as every look discloses
I hoped for; never hoped to earn.

Damnation, dawn already! This is
Our darkest moment, parting so.
The world of rapture in your kisses!
But in your eye, the worlds of woe!
I left—your look, though lowered, stealing
Its tearful glances by the gate.
Yet being loved! It's great, the feeling!
And loving—! God above, it's great!

John Frederick Nims

Autumn, 1775

Green more greenly, you leaves
On the grape-vined wall,
Upwards here to my window.
Tighten your skins tighter still,
Twinned clusters, ripen faster

Schneller und glänzend voller.
Euch brütet der Mutter Sonne
Scheideblick, euch umsäuselt
Des holden Himmels
Fruchtende Fülle.
Euch kühlet des Monds
Freundlicher Zauberhauch,
Und euch betauen, ach,
Aus diesen Augen
Der ewig belebenden Liebe
Voll schwellende Tränen.

Prometheus

Bedecke deinen Himmel, Zeus,
Mit Wolkendunst!
Und übe, dem Knaben gleich,
Der Disteln köpft,
An Eichen dich und Bergeshöhn!
Mußt mir meine Erde
Doch lassen stehn,
Und meine Hütte,
Die du nicht gebaut,
Und meinen Herd,
Um dessen Glut
Du mich beneidest.

Ich kenne nichts Ärmeres
Unter der Sonn als euch Götter.
Ihr nähret kümmerlich
Von Opfersteuern
Und Gebetshauch
Eure Majestät
Und darbtet, wären
Nicht Kinder und Bettler
Hoffnungsvolle Toren.

And lustrously fuller.
Brooding rays of Mother Sun's
Parting glance warm you,
Kind heaven's fructifying fulness
Whispers about you,
The friendly moon's magic breath
Cools you, and, o,
From these eyes
Ever animating love's
Full swelling tears
Bedew you.

R. M. Browning

Prometheus

Cover your heaven, Zeus,
With cloudy vapors
And like a boy
Beheading thistles
Practice on oaks and mountain peaks—
Still you must leave
My earth intact
And my small hovel, which you did not build,
And this my hearth
Whose glowing heat
You envy me.

I know of nothing more wretched
Under the sun than you gods!
Meagerly you nourish
Your majesty
On dues of sacrifice
And breath of prayer
And would suffer want
But for children and beggars,
Poor hopeful fools.

Da ich ein Kind war,
Nicht wußte, wo aus noch ein,
Kehrte mein verirrtes Auge
Zur Sonne, als wenn drüber wär'
Ein Ohr, zu hören meine Klage,
Ein Herz wie meines,
Sich des Bedrängten zu erbarmen.

Wer half mir
Wider der Titanen Übermut?
Wer rettete vom Tode mich,
Von Sklaverei?
Hast du's nicht alles selbst vollendet,
Heilig glühend Herz?
Und glühtest, jung und gut,
Betrogen, Rettungsdank
Dem Schlafenden dadroben?

Ich dich ehren? Wofür?
Hast du die Schmerzen gelindert
Je des Beladenen?
Hast du die Tränen gestillet
Je des Geängsteten?
Hat nicht mich zum Manne geschmiedet
Die allmächtige Zeit
Und das ewige Schicksal,
Meine Herrn und deine?

Wähntest du etwa,
Ich sollte das Leben hassen,
In Wüsten fliehn,
Weil nicht alle
Blütenträume reiften?

Hier sitz' ich, forme Menschen
Nach meinem Bilde,
Ein Geschlecht, das mir gleich sei,
Zu leiden, zu weinen,

Once too, a child
Not knowing where to turn,
I raised bewildered eyes
Up to the sun, as if above there were
An ear to hear my complaint,
A heart like mine
To take pity on the oppressed.

Who helped me
Against the Titans' arrogance?
Who rescued me from death,
From slavery?
Did not my holy and glowing heart,
Unaided, accomplish all?
And did it not, young and good,
Cheated, glow thankfulness
For its safety to him, to the sleeper above?

I pay homage to you? For what?
Have you ever relieved
The burdened man's anguish?
Have you ever assuaged
The frightened man's tears?
Was it not omnipotent Time
That forged me into manhood,
And eternal Fate,
My masters and yours?

Or did you think perhaps
That I should hate this life,
Flee into deserts
Because not all
The blossoms of dream grew ripe?

Here I sit, forming men
In my image,
A race to resemble me:
To suffer, to weep,

Zu genießen und zu freuen sich,
Und dein nicht zu achten,
Wie ich.

Mahomets Gesang

Seht den Felsenquell
Freudehell,
Wie ein Sternenblick!
Über Wolken
Nährten seine Jugend
Gute Geister
Zwischen Klippen im Gebüsch.

Jünglingfrisch
Tanzt er aus der Wolke
Auf die Marmorfelsen nieder,
Jauchzet wieder
Nach dem Himmel.
Durch die Gipfelgänge
Jagt er bunten Kieseln nach,
Und mit frühem Führertritt
Reißt er seine Bruderquellen
Mit sich fort.

Drunten werden in dem Tal
Unter seinem Fußtritt Blumen,
Und die Wiese
Lebt von seinem Hauch.
Doch ihn hält kein Schattental,
Keine Blumen,
Die ihm seine Knie' umschlingen,
Ihm mit Liebesaugen schmeicheln;

To enjoy, to be glad—
And never to heed you,
Like me!

Michael Hamburger

A Song to Mahomet

See the mountain spring
Flash gladdening
Like a glance of stars;
Higher than the clouds
Kindly spirits
Fuelled his youth
In thickets twixt the crags.

Brisk as a young blade
Out of cloud he dances
Down to marble rocks
And leaps again
Skyward exultant.
Down passages that hang from peaks
He chases pebbles many-coloured,
Early like a leader striding
Snatches up and carries onward
Brother torrents.

Flowers are born beneath his footprint
In the valley down below,
From his breathing
Pastures live.
Yet no valley of the shadows
Can contain him
And no flowers that clasp his knees,
Blandishing with looks of love;

Nach der Ebne dringt sein Lauf,
Schlangenwandelnd.

Bäche schmiegen
Sich gesellig an.
Nun tritt er
In die Ebne silberprangend,
Und die Ebne prangt mit ihm,
Und die Flüsse von der Ebne
Und die Bäche von den Bergen
Jauchzen ihm und rufen: Bruder!
Bruder, nimm die Brüder mit,
Mit zu deinem alten Vater,
Zu dem ew'gen Ozean,
Der mit ausgespannten Armen
Unsrer wartet;
Die sich, ach, vergebens öffnen,
Seine Sehnenden zu fassen;
Denn uns frißt in öder Wüste
Gier'ger Sand,
Die Sonne droben
Saugt an unserm Blut,
Ein Hügel
Hemmet uns zum Teiche.
Bruder,
Nimm die Brüder von der Ebne,
Nimm die Brüder von den Bergen
Mit, zu deinem Vater mit!

Kommt ihr alle!—
Und nun schwillt er
Herrlicher, ein ganz Geschlechte
Trägt den Fürsten hoch empor,
Und im rollenden Triumphe
Gibt er Ländern Namen, Städte
Werden unter seinem Fuß.

Unaufhaltsam rauscht er weiter,
Läßt der Türe Flammengipfel,

To the lowland bursts his way,
A snake uncoiling.

Freshets nestle
Flocking to his side. He comes
Into the lowland, silver sparkling
And with him the lowland sparkles,
And the lowland rivers call,
Mountain freshets call exultant:
Brother, take your brothers with you,
With you to your ancient father,
To the everlasting ocean,
Who with open arms awaits us,
Arms which, ah, open in vain
To clasp us who are craving for him;
Avid sand consumes us
In the desert, sun overhead
Will suck our blood, blocked by a hill
To pools we shrink! Brother, take us,
Take your lowland brothers with you,
Take your brothers of the mountains,
To your father take us all!

Join me then!
And now he swells
More lordly still; one single kin,
They loft the prince and bear him high
Onward as he rolls triumphant,
Naming countries, in his track
Towns and cities come to be.

On he rushes, unrelenting,
Leaves the turrets tipped with flame,

Marmorhäuser, eine Schöpfung
Seiner Fülle, hinter sich.

Zedernhäuser trägt der Atlas
Auf den Riesenschultern, sausend
Wehen über seinem Haupte
Tausend Segel durch die Lüfte
Zeugen seiner Herrlichkeit.

Und so trägt er seine Brüder,
Seine Schätze, seine Kinder
Dem erwartenden Erzeuger
Freudebrausend an das Herz.

Auf dem See

Und frische Nahrung, neues Blut
Saug ich aus freier Welt;
Wie ist Natur so hold und gut,
Die mich am Busen hält!
Die Welle wieget unsern Kahn
Im Rudertakt hinauf,
Und Berge, wolkig himmelan,
Begegnen unserm Lauf.

Aug', mein Aug', was sinkst du nieder?
Goldne Träume, kommt ihr wieder?
Weg, du Traum, so gold du bist:
Hier auch Lieb' und Leben ist.

Auf der Welle blinken
Tausend schwebende Sterne,
Weiche Nebel trinken
Rings die türmende Ferne;

Marble palaces, creation
Of his plenitude, behind him.

Cedar houses he like Atlas
Carries on his giant shoulders;
Flags a thousand rustling flutter
In the air above his head,
Testifying to his glory.

So he bears his brothers, bears
His treasures and his children surging
In a wave of joy tumultuous
To their waiting father's heart.

Christopher Middleton

On the Lake

My blood flows fresh, my soul finds food,
    I roam the world at large;
And Nature,—smiles she not most good?
    She holds my heart in charge.
The wavelets lift our little boat,
    With the oars, in measured beat,
And hills, piled cloudlike, hither float
    Our bounding bark to meet.

Eye, mine eye, why art thou sinking?
Of those dreams must still be thinking?
    Go, Dream! golden as thou art;
    Here, too, love and life have part.

Under the wave fly, blinking,
    Shoals of stars, as I ponder;
Flocks of clouds hang drinking
    Round the hills away yonder:

Morgenwind umflügelt
Die beschattete Bucht,
Und im See bespiegelt
Sich die reifende Frucht.

An den Mond

Füllest wieder Busch und Tal
Still mit Nebelglanz,
Lösest endlich auch einmal
Meine Seele ganz;

Breitest über mein Gefild
Lindernd deinen Blick,
Wie des Freundes Auge mild
Über mein Geschick.

Jeden Nachklang fühlt mein Herz
Froh- und trüber Zeit,
Wandle zwischen Freud und Schmerz
In der Einsamkeit.

Fließe, fließe, lieber Fluß!
Nimmer werd ich froh,
So verrauschte Scherz und Kuß,
Und die Treue so.

Ich besaß es doch einmal,
Was so köstlich ist!
Daß man doch zu seiner Qual
Nimmer es vergißt!

Rausche, Fluß, das Tal entlang,
Ohne Rast und Ruh,
Rausche, flüstre meinem Sang
Melodien zu,

Morning wind is dancing
  O'er the shadowy cove,
From the lake come glancing
  Fruits half hid in the grove.

J. S. Dwight

To the Moon

[handwritten: In German, Moon is masculine]

Flooding with a brilliant mist
Valley, bush and tree,
You release me. Oh for once
Heart and soul I'm free!

Easy on the region round
Goes your wider gaze,
Like a friend's indulgent eye
Measuring my days.

Every echo from the past,
Glum or gaudy mood,
Haunts me—weighing bliss and pain
In the solitude.

River, flow and flow away;
Pleasure's dead to me:
Gone the laughing kisses, gone
Lips and loyalty.

All in my possession once!
Such a treasure yet
Any man would pitch in pain
Rather than forget.

Water, rush along the pass,
Never lag at ease;
Rush, and rustle to my song
Changing melodies,

Wenn du in der Winternacht
Wütend überschwillst,
Oder um die Frühlingspracht
Junger Knospen quillst.

Selig, wer sich vor der Welt
Ohne Haß verschließt,
Einen Freund am Busen hält
Und mit dem genießt,

Was, von Menschen nicht gewußt
Oder nicht bedacht,
Durch das Labyrinth der Brust
Wandelt in der Nacht.

Grenzen der Menschheit

Wenn der uralte
Heilige Vater
Mit gelassener Hand
Aus rollenden Wolken
Segnende Blitze
Über die Erde sät
Küss' ich den letzten
Saum seines Kleides,
Kindliche Schauer
Treu in der Brust.

Denn mit Göttern
Soll sich nicht messen
Irgend ein Mensch.
Hebt er sich aufwärts
Und berührt
Mit dem Scheitel die Sterne,
Nirgends haften dann
Die unsichern Sohlen,

How in dark December you
Roll amok in flood;
Curling, in the gala May,
Under branch and bud.

Happy man, that rancor-free
Shows the world his door;
One companion by—and both
In a glow before

Something never guessed by men
Or rejected quite:
Which, in mazes of the breast,
Wanders in the night.

John Frederick Nims

Human Limits

When the most ancient
Heavenly Father
From rolling clouds
With a calm hand scatters
Lightning flashes like seed
Over the earth,
I kiss the lowest
Hem of his garment,
A childlike awe
Steadfast within me.

For against gods
No man alive
Should measure himself.
If he rises up
And with the crown of his head
Touches the stars,
Nowhere then do the groping
Soles of his feet adhere,

Und mit ihm spielen
Wolken und Winde.

Steht er mit festen,
Markigen Knochen
Auf der wohlgegründeten
Dauernden Erde,
Reicht er nicht auf,
Nur mit der Eiche
Oder der Rebe
Sich zu vergleichen.

Was unterscheidet
Götter von Menschen?
Daß viele Wellen
Vor jenen wandeln,
Ein ewiger Strom:
Uns hebt die Welle,
Verschlingt die Welle,
Und wir versinken.

Ein kleiner Ring
Begrenzt unser Leben,
Und viele Geschlechter
Reihen sich dauernd
An ihres Daseins
Unendliche Kette.

Wandrers Nachtlied

Der du von dem Himmel bist,
Alles Leid und Schmerzen stillest,
Den, der doppelt elend ist,
Doppelt mit Erquickung füllest,

But clouds and winds
Make him their game.

[handwritten: at the mercy of nature]

If with firm,
Marrowy bones he stands
On the well-founded
Durable earth,
Not with so much as the oak
Or the vine
He can presume
To compare his height.

What distinguishes
Gods from human kind?
That many waves
Move before gods,
An eternal tide;
Us the wave lifts,
Us the wave engulfs,
And we go down.

[handwritten: pos. ov wlg.?]

A little ring
Confines our lives,
And many generations
For ever they link
On to their being's
Infinite chain.

[handwritten: 'Man' is infinite?]

Michael Hamburger

Wanderer's Night-Songs

I

Thou that from the heavens art,
Every pain and sorrow stillest,
And the doubly wretched heart
Doubly with refreshment fillest,

—Ach, ich bin des Treibens müde,
Was soll all der Schmerz und Lust?—
Süßer Friede,
Komm, ach komm in meine Brust!

Ein Gleiches

Über allen Gipfeln
Ist Ruh,
In allen Wipfeln
Spürest du
Kaum einen Hauch;
Die Vögelein schweigen im Walde.
Warte nur, balde
Ruhest du auch.

Mignon

I

Kennst du das Land, wo die Zitronen blühn,
Im dunkeln Laub die Gold-Orangen glühn,
Ein sanfter Wind vom blauen Himmel weht,
Die Myrte still und hoch der Lorbeer steht,
Kennst du es wohl?
                    Dahin! Dahin
Möcht ich mit dir, o mein Geliebter, ziehn.

Kennst du das Haus? Auf Säulen ruht sein Dach,
Es glänzt der Saal, es schimmert das Gemach,
Und Marmorbilder stehn und sehn mich an:
Was hat man dir, du armes Kind, getan?
Kennst du es wohl?
                    Dahin! Dahin
Möcht ich mit dir, o mein Beschützer, ziehn.

Kennst du den Berg und seinen Wolkensteg?
Das Maultier sucht im Nebel seinen Weg,

I am weary with contending!
Why this rapture and unrest?
Peace descending
Come, ah, come into my breast!

II

O'er all the hill-tops
Is quiet now,
In all the tree-tops
Hearest thou
Hardly a breath;
The birds are asleep in the trees:
Wait; soon like these
Thou too shalt rest.

H. W. Longfellow

Mignon

You know that land, her lemon groves in bloom?
Dark foliage of the orange, gold in gloom?
So soft a blowing air, so blue a sky
Over the myrtle hushed, the laurel high?
You know that land perhaps?
                    Oh that's the way
I'd go with you, my dearest—off today!

You know that house, how tall the pillars stand?
The halls all glossy, and the chambers grand?
The marble shapes that eye me, where I go:
"What's the world done, poor child, to hurt you so?"
You know the house perhaps?
                    Oh that's the way
I'd go with you, my guardian—off today!

You know that mountain and its cloudy track?
The drifting haze, the mule-clop echoing back?

In Höhlen wohnt der Drachen alte Brut,
Es stürzt der Fels und über ihn die Flut;
Kennst du ihn wohl?
                    Dahin! Dahin
Geht unser Weg! o Vater, laß uns ziehn!

II

Nur wer die Sehnsucht kennt,
Weiß, was ich leide!
Allein und abgetrennt
Von aller Freude,
Seh' ich ans Firmament
Nach jener Seite.
Ach! der mich liebt und kennt,
Ist in der Weite.
Es schwindelt mir, es brennt
Mein Eingeweide.
Nur wer die Sehnsucht kennt,
Weiß, was ich leide.

Alles geben die Götter, die unendlichen,
Ihren Lieblingen ganz,
Alle Freuden, die unendlichen,
Alle Schmerzen, die unendlichen, ganz.

—Old dragons and their brood in grottoes sprawl;
Each rock's a cliff; each brook, a waterfall.
You know the place perhaps?
                              Oh that's the way
Our journey goes! Good father, off today!

John Frederick Nims

Who Yearning Knows

Only who yearning knows
Knows my bereavement.

Shut here within my sorrows
Of joyless banishment
I watch a great sky close
There where he went.
Ah, he who loves and knows
Me is now distant.
This burns, the searing grows
Through my heart rent.

Only who yearning knows
Knows my bereavement.

Stephen Spender

The Gods Give Everything

The gods give everything, the infinite ones,
To their beloved, completely,
Every pleasure, the infinite ones,
Every suffering, the infinite ones, completely.

Stephen Spender

Anakreons Grab

Wo die Rose hier blüht, wo Reben um Lorbeer sich schlingen,
  Wo das Turtelchen lockt, wo sich das Grillchen ergetzt,
Welch ein Grab ist hier, das all Götter mit Leben
  Schön bepflanzt und geziert? Es ist Anakreons Ruh.
Frühling, Sommer und Herbst genoß der glückliche Dichter;
  Vor dem Winter hat ihn endlich der Hügel geschützt.

Natur und Kunst

Natur und Kunst, sie scheinen sich zu fliehen
Und haben sich, eh man es denkt, gefunden;
Der Widerwille ist auch mir verschwunden,
Und beide scheinen gleich mich anzuziehen.

Es gilt wohl nur ein redliches Bemühen!
Und wenn wir erst in abgemeßnen Stunden
Mit Geist und Fleiß uns an die Kunst gebunden,
Mag frei Natur im Herzen wieder glühen.

So ists mit aller Bildung auch beschaffen.
Vergebens werden ungebundne Geister
Nach der Vollendung reiner Höhe streben.

Wer Großes will, muß sich zusammenraffen.
In der Beschränkung zeigt sich erst der Meister,
Und das Gesetz nur kann uns Freiheit geben.

Anacreon's Grave

Where the rose is in flower, where vines interlace with the laurel,
  Where the turtle-dove calls, where the small cricket delights,
What a grave is this, which all the gods have embellished,
  Graced and planted with life? It is Anacreon's rest.
Springtime, summer, and autumn blessed the fortunate poet:
  And from winter the mound kept him secure in the end.

Michael Hamburger

Sonnet

Nature, it seems, must always clash with Art,
And yet, before we know it, both are one;
I too have learnt: their enmity is none,
Since each compels me, and in equal part.

Hard, honest work counts most! And once we start
To measure out the hours and never shun
Art's daily labor till our task is done,
Freely again may Nature move the heart.

So too all growth and ripening of the mind:
To the pure heights of ultimate consummation
In vain the unbound spirit seeks to flee.

Who seeks great gain leaves easy gain behind.
None proves a master but by limitation
And only law can give us liberty.

Michael Hamburger

Gefunden

Ich ging im Walde
So für mich hin,
Und nichts zu suchen,
Das war mein Sinn.

Im Schatten sah ich
Ein Blümchen stehn,
Wie Sterne leuchtend,
Wie Äuglein schön.

Ich wollt es brechen,
Da sagt' es fein:
Soll ich zum Welken
Gebrochen sein?

Ich grub's mit allen
Den Würzlein aus,
Zum Garten trug ich's
Am hübschen Haus.

Und pflanzt' es wieder
Am stillen Ort;
Nun zweigt es immer
Und blüht so fort.

Wiederfinden

Ist es möglich! Stern der Sterne,
Drück' ich wieder dich ans Herz!
Ach, was ist die Nacht der Ferne
Für ein Abgrund, für ein Schmerz!
Ja, du bist es! meiner Freuden

In a Glade

In a glade
  I idly went,
Nought to seek
  Was my intent.

I saw a flower
  In shelter shy,
Fair as a star,
  Sweet as an eye.

I stoop'd to pluck it,
  Then did it say:
"Why be gather'd
  To fade away?"

I gently loosed
  The earth around,
Bore it home to my
  Garden-ground.

In a nook
  The flower I set,
There it grows and
  Blossoms yet.

Richard Garnett

Reunion

Star of stars, O can it be,
I press you to my heart again!
What a chasm is the night
Of being far apart, what pain!
Yes, it is you, of all my joys

Süßer, lieber Widerpart;
Eingedenk vergangner Leiden,
Schaudr' ich vor der Gegenwart.

Als die Welt im tiefsten Grunde
Lag an Gottes ew'ger Brust,
Ordnet' er die erste Stunde
Mit erhabner Schöpfungslust,
Und er sprach das Wort: ‚Es werde!'
Da erklang ein schmerzlich Ach!
Als das All mit Machtgebärde
In die Wirklichkeiten brach.

Auf tat sich das Licht! So trennte
Scheu sich Finsternis von ihm,
Und sogleich die Elemente
Scheidend auseinander fliehn.
Rasch, in wilden, wüsten Träumen
Jedes nach der Weite rang,
Starr, in ungemeßnen Räumen,
Ohne Sehnsucht, ohne Klang.

Stumm war alles, still und öde,
Einsam Gott zum erstenmal!
Da erschuf er Morgenröte,
Die erbarmte sich der Qual;
Sie entwickelte dem Trüben
Ein erklingend Farbenspiel,
Und nun konnte wieder lieben,
Was erst auseinander fiel.

Und mit eiligem Bestreben
Sucht sich, was sich angehört,
Und zu ungemeßnem Leben
Ist Gefühl und Blick gekehrt.
Sei's Ergreifen, sei es Raffen,
Wenn es nur sich faßt und hält!
Allah braucht nicht mehr zu schaffen,
Wir erschaffen seine Welt.

The dearest image, sweetest rhyme.
Bygone suffering I recall
And shudder at the present time.

When the world lay in the depths
Utmost of God's eternal breast,
Creative with delight sublime
He willed a moment to be first;
As he spoke the word "Become!",
An anguished "Ah!" rang out, the All
Exploded with a motion vast
Into being actual.

Light was opened wide: the dark
Withdrew from it with diffidence;
Separation, scattering
Clove then apart the elements.
Quickly each in savage dreams
And desolate its distance found,
Stiffened in unmeasured space
Without longing, without sound.

All was void, and mute, and still,
God's first taste of solitude.
Then he made the rose of dawn,
Pity on the pain she strewed,
So inventing for the dark,
Of hues and harmonies a game,
And everything that fell apart
Now could fall in love again.

Beings, if they do belong,
Each seeks the other in its place;
Sight and feeling hurtle them
Back to life that's measureless.
Grasp or snatch, no matter how,
Take hold they must, if they're to be:
Allah's work for now is done,
Creators of his world are we.

So, mit morgenroten Flügeln,
Riß es mich an deinen Mund,
Und die Nacht mit tausend Siegeln
Kräftigt sternenhell den Bund.
Beide sind wir auf der Erde
Musterhaft in Freud' und Qual,
Und ein zweites Wort: Es werde!
Trennt uns nicht zum zweitenmal.

Proœmion

Im Namen dessen, der Sich selbst erschuf!
Von Ewigkeit in schaffendem Beruf;
In Seinem Namen, der den Glauben schafft,
Vertrauen, Liebe, Tätigkeit und Kraft;
In Jenes Namen, der, so oft genannt,
Dem Wesen nach blieb immer unbekannt:

So weit das Ohr, so weit das Auge reicht,
Du findest nur Bekanntes, das Ihm gleicht,
Und deines Geistes höchster Feuerflug
Hat schon am Gleichnis, hat am Bild genug;
Es zieht dich an, es reißt dich heiter fort,
Und wo du wandelst, schmückt sich Weg und Ort;
Du zählst nicht mehr, berechnest keine Zeit,
Und jeder Schritt ist Unermeßlichkeit.

Was wär' ein Gott, der nur von außen stieße,
Im Kreis das All am Finger laufen ließe!
Ihm ziemt's, die Welt im Innern zu bewegen,
Natur in Sich, Sich in Natur zu hegen,
So daß, was in Ihm lebt und webt und ist,
Nie Seine Kraft, nie Seinen Geist vermißt.

Thus on wings of rosy dawn
To your lips I flew and fly,
Starbright with a thousand seals
Night the bond will ratify.
Together on the earth we stand,
Exemplars both, in joy and pain,
And a second word "Become!"
Shall not tear us apart again.

Christopher Middleton

Prooemion

In His blest name, who was His own creation,
Who from all time makes *making* His vocation;
The name of Him who makes our faith so bright,
Love, confidence, activity, and might;
In that One's name, who, named though oft He be,
Unknown is ever in Reality:

As far as ear can reach, or eyesight dim,
Thou findest but the known resembling Him;
How high soe'er thy fiery spirit hovers,
Its simile and type it straight discovers;
Onward thou'rt drawn, with feelings light and gay,
Where e'er thou goest, smiling is the way;
No more thou numberest, reckonest no time,
Each step is infinite, each step sublime.

What God would *outwardly* alone control,
And on His finger whirl the mighty Whole?
He loves the *inner* world to move, to view
Nature in Him, Himself in Nature, too,
So that what in Him works, and is, and lives,
The measure of His strength, His spirit gives.

Im Innern ist ein Universum auch;
Daher der Völker löblicher Gebrauch,
Daß jeglicher das Beste, was er kennt,
Er Gott, ja seinen Gott benennt,
Ihm Himmel und Erden übergibt,
Ihm fürchtet und womöglich liebt.

Urworte, Orphisch

Daimon, Dämon

Wie an dem Tag, der dich der Welt verliehen,
Die Sonne stand zum Gruße der Planeten,
Bist alsobald und fort und fort gediehen
Nach dem Gesetz, wonach du angetreten.
So mußt du sein, dir kannst du nicht entfliehen,
So sagten schon Sibyllen, so Propheten;
Und keine Zeit und keine Macht zerstückelt
Geprägte Form, die lebend sich entwickelt.

Tyche, Das Zufällige

Die strenge Grenze doch umgeht gefällig
Ein Wandelndes, das mit und um uns wandelt;
Nicht einsam bleibst du, bildest dich gesellig
Und handelst wohl so, wie ein andrer handelt.
Im Leben ists bald hin-, bald widerfällig,
Es ist ein Tand und wird so durchgetandelt.
Schon hat sich still der Jahre Kreis geründet,
Die Lampe harrt der Flamme, die entzündet.

Eros, Liebe

Die bleibt nicht aus!—Er stürzt vom Himmel nieder,
Wohin er sich aus alter Öde schwang,
Er schwebt heran auf luftigem Gefieder

Within us all a universe doth dwell;
And hence each people's usage laudable,
That every one the Best that meets his eyes
As God, yea, e'en *his* God, doth recognize;
To Him both earth and heaven surrenders he,
Fears Him, and loves Him, too, if that may be.

E. A. Bowring

Primeval Words, Orphic

Daimon

As on the day in which your life began
The sun to stars and planets was related,
So you unfolded, following a plan
Determined on the day you were created.
Thus you must be, escape you never can,
Sibyls and prophets long ago thus stated.
And neither time nor force can ever break
The finished form that growing life will take.

Chance

These strict confines are softly bypassed, though,
By change that changes with us as we stride.
You do not stay alone; with friends you come and go,
You act indeed like others by your side.
Life brings adjustment, motion to and fro—
It is an idle ride, and so you ride.
Soon year and year in rounding chain combine,
The lamp awaits the spark, to make it shine.

Love

And it will come! Down from the sky he flings
Himself, to which from earthly dust he rose.
He floats along upon his airy wings;

Um Stirn und Brust den Frühlingstag entlang,
Scheint jetzt zu fliehn, vom Fliehen kehrt er wieder:
Da wird ein Wohl im Weh, so süß und bang.
Gar manches Herz verschwebt im Allgemeinen,
Doch widmet sich das edelste dem Einen.

Ananke, Nötigung

Da ists denn wieder, wie die Sterne wollten:
Bedingung und Gesetz, und aller Wille
Ist nur ein Wollen, weil wir eben sollten,
Und vor dem Willen schweigt die Willkür stille;
Das Liebste wird vom Herzen weggescholten,
Dem harten Muß bequemt sich Will und Grille.
So sind wir scheinfrei denn, nach manchen Jahren
Nur enger dran, als wir am Anfang waren.

Elpis, Hoffnung

Doch solcher Grenze, solcher ehrnen Mauer
Höchst widerwärt'ge Pforte wird entriegelt,
Sie stehe nur mit alter Felsendauer!
Ein Wesen regt sich leicht und ungezügelt:
Aus Wolkendecke, Nebel, Regenschauer
Erhebt sie uns, mit ihr, durch sie beflügelt,
Ihr kennt sie wohl, sie schwärmt durch alle Zonen—
Ein Flügelschlag—und hinter uns Äonen!

Selige Sehnsucht

Sagt es niemand, nur den Weisen,
Weil die Menge gleich verhöhnet,
Das Lebend'ge will ich preisen,
Das nach Flammentod sich sehnet.

In der Liebesnächte Kühlung,
Die dich zeugte, wo du zeugtest,

Around his head and breast a spring day flows.
He seems to flee, then back from flight he swings,
While bliss from pain, or joy from anguish, grows.
The hearts of many men may hither float, or yon;
The noblest heart, however, stays with one.

Necessity

There 'tis again—the planets' whim, anew:
All regulations, laws, and every will
Are only willed as something we must do.
Where will prevails, caprice must come to nil;
Your heart's desires shall be withheld from you,
And that which Must commands, Will must fulfill.
Thus freedom—an illusion of the heart—
Has, after years, more limits than at start.

Hope

The gate, though, in this wall of limitation,
Shall soon be opened up—that hateful gate!
Let it but stand upon its firm foundation!
A spirit rises from it, free and straight.
She lifts us on her wings to liberation;
From clouds and mist toward a better fate.
Familiar is her flight, and to no land confined;
One stroke of wings—and eons lie behind!

Max Knight and Joseph Fabry

 Blessed Longing

Tell it only to the wise,
For the crowd at once will jeer:
That which is alive I praise,
That which longs for death by fire.

Cooled by passionate love at night,
Procreated, procreating,

Überfällt dich fremde Fühlung,
Wenn die stille Kerze leuchtet.

Nicht mehr bleibest du umfangen
In der Finsternis Beschattung,
Und dich reißet neu Verlangen
Auf zu höherer Begattung.

Keine Ferne macht dich schwierig,
Kommst geflogen und gebannt,
Und zuletzt, des Lichts begierig,
Bist du, Schmetterling, verbrannt.

Und so lang du das nicht hast,
Dieses: Stirb und werde!
Bist du nur ein trüber Gast
Auf der dunklen Erde.

Dauer im Wechsel

Hielte diesen frühen Segen,
Ach, nur *eine* Stunde fest!
Aber vollen Blütenregen
Schüttelt schon der laue West.
Soll ich mich des Grünen freuen,
Dem ich Schatten erst verdankt?
Bald wird Sturm auch das zerstreuen,
Wenn es falb im Herbst geschwankt.

Willst du nach den Früchten greifen,
Eilig nimm dein Teil davon!
Diese fangen an zu reifen,
Und die andern keimen schon;
Gleich mit jedem Regengusse
Ändert sich dein holdes Tal,
Ach, und in demselben Flusse
Schwimmst du nicht zum zweitenmal.

You have known the alien feeling
In the calm of candlelight;

Gloom-embraced will lie no more,
By the flickering shades obscured,
But are seized by new desire,
To a higher union lured.

Then no distance holds you fast;
Winged, enchanted, on you fly,
Light your longing, and at last,
Moth, you meet the flame and die.

Never prompted to that quest:
Die and dare rebirth!
You remain a dreary guest
On our gloomy earth.

Michael Hamburger

*The classic
Goethe
quote*

Permanence in Change

Early blossoms—could a single
Hour preserve them just as now!
But the warmer west will scatter
Petals showering from the bough.
How enjoy these leaves, that lately
I was grateful to for shade?
Soon the wind and snow are rolling
What the late Novembers fade.

Fruit—you'd reach a hand and have it?
Better have it then with speed.
These you see about to ripen,
Those already gone to seed.
Half a rainy day, and there's your
Pleasant valley not the same.
None could swim that very river
Twice, so quick the changes came.

Du nun selbst! Was felsenfeste
Sich von dir hervorgetan,
Mauern siehst du, siehst Paläste
Stets mit andern Augen an.
Weggeschwunden ist die Lippe,
Die im Kusse sonst genas,
Jener Fuß, der an der Klippe
Sich mit Gemsenfreche maß.

Jene Hand, die gern und milde
Sich bewegte wohlzutun,
Das gegliederte Gebilde,
Alles ist ein andres nun.
Und was sich an jener Stelle
Nun mit deinem Namen nennt,
Kam herbei wie eine Welle,
Und so eilt's zum Element.

Laß den Anfang mit dem Ende
Sich in eins zusammenziehn!
Schneller als die Gegenstände
Selber dich vorüberfliehn.
Danke, daß die Gunst der Musen
Unvergängliches verheißt,
Den Gehalt in deinem Busen
Und die Form in deinem Geist.

You yourself! What all around you
Strong as stonework used to lie
—Castles, battlements—you see them
With an ever-changing eye.
Now the lips are dim and withered
Once the kisses set aglow;
Lame the leg, that on the mountain
Left the mountain goat below.

Or that hand, that knew such loving
Ways, outstretching in caress,
—Cunningly adjusted structure—
Now can function less and less.
All are gone; this substitution
Has your name and nothing more.
Like a wave it lifts and passes,
Back to atoms on the shore.

See in each beginning, ending,
Double aspects of the One;
Here, amid stampeding objects,
Be among the first to run,
Thankful to a muse whose favor
Grants you one unchanging thing:
What the heart can hold to ponder;
What the spirit shape to sing.

John Frederick Nims

Friedrich Schiller

Dithyrambe

Nimmer, das glaubt mir,
Erscheinen die Götter,
Nimmer allein.
Kaum daß ich Bacchus, den lustigen, habe,
Kommt auch schon Amor, der lächelnde Knabe,
Phöbus der Herrliche findet sich ein.
Sie nahen, sie kommen
Die Himmlischen alle,
Mit Göttern erfüllt sich
Die irdische Halle.

Sagt, wie bewirt ich,
Der Erdegeborne,
Himmlischen Chor?
Schenket mir euer unsterbliches Leben,
Götter! Was kann euch der Sterbliche geben?
Hebet zu eurem Olymp mich empor!
Die Freude, sie wohnt nur
In Jupiters Saale,
O füllet mit Nektar,
O reicht mir die Schale!

Reich ihm die Schale!
Schenke dem Dichter,
Hebe, nur ein.
Netz ihm die Augen mit himmlischem Taue,
Daß er den Styx, den verhaßten, nicht schaue,
Einer der Unsern sich dünke zu sein.
Sie rauschet, sie perlet,
Die himmlische Quelle,
Der Busen wird ruhig,
Das Auge wird helle.

Friedrich Schiller

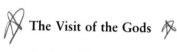 **The Visit of the Gods**

(Imitated from Schiller)

> Never, believe me,
> Appear the Immortals,
> Never alone:
> Scarce had I welcomed the sorrow-beguiler,
> Iacchus! but in came boy Cupid the smiler;
> Lo! Phoebus the glorious descends from his throne!
> They advance, they float in, the Olympians all!
> With divinities fills my
> Terrestrial hall!

Earthly?

> How shall I yield you
> Due entertainment,
> Celestial quire?
> Me rather, bright guests! with your wings of upbuoyance,
> Bear aloft to your homes, to your banquets of joyance,
> That the roofs of Olympus may echo my lyre!
> Hah! we mount! on their pinions they waft up my soul!
> O give me the nectar!
> O fill me the bowl!

> Give him the nectar!
> Pour out for the poet,
> Hebe! pour free!
> Quicken his eyes with celestial dew,
> That Styx the detested no more he may view,
> And like one of us Gods may conceit him to be!
> Thanks, Hebe! I quaff it! Io Paean, I cry!
> The wine of the Immortals
> Forbids me to die!

Samuel Taylor Coleridge

Des Mädchens Klage

Der Eichwald brauset,
Die Wolken ziehn,
Das Mägdlein sitzet
An Ufers Grün,
Es bricht sich die Welle mit Macht, mit Macht,
Und sie seufzt hinaus in die finstre Nacht,
Das Auge vom Weinen getrübet.

»Das Herz ist gestorben,
Die Welt ist leer,
Und weiter gibt sie
Dem Wunsche nichts mehr.
Du Heilige, rufe dein Kind zurück,
Ich habe genossen das irdische Glück,
Ich habe gelebt und geliebet!«

Es rinnet der Tränen
Vergeblicher Lauf,
Die Klage, sie wecket
Die Toten nicht auf,
Doch nenne, was tröstet und heilet die Brust
Nach der süßen Liebe verschwundener Lust,
Ich, die himmlische, wills nicht versagen.

»Laß rinnen der Tränen
Vergeblichen Lauf,
Es wecke die Klage
Den Toten nicht auf,
Das süßeste Glück für die traurende Brust,
Nach der schönen Liebe verschwundener Lust,
Sind der Liebe Schmerzen und Klagen.«

The Maiden's Plaint

The forestpines groan—
The dim clouds are flitting—
The Maiden is sitting
On the green shore alone.
The surges are broken with might, with might,
And her sighs are pour'd on the desert Night,
And tears are troubling her eye.

"All, all is o'er:
The heart is destroyed—
The world is a void—
It can yield me no more.
Then, Master of Life, take back thy boon:
I have tasted such bliss as is under the moon:
I have lived—I have loved—I would die!"

Thy tears, O Forsaken!
Are gushing in vain;
Thy wail shall not waken
The Buried again:
But all that is left for the desolate bosom,
The flower of whose Love has been blasted in blossom,
Be granted to thee from on high!

Then pour like a river
Thy tears without number!
The Buried can never
Be wept from their slumber:
But the luxury dear to the Broken-hearted,
When the sweet enchantment of Love hath departed,
Be thine—the tear and the sigh!

James Clarence Mangan

Der Ring des Polykrates

Er stand auf seines Daches Zinnen,
Er schaute mit vergnügten Sinnen
Auf das beherrschte Samos hin.
»Dies alles ist mir untertänig«,
Begann er zu Ägyptens König,
»Gestehe, das ich glücklich bin.«

»Du hast der Götter Gunst erfahren!
Die vormals deinesgleichen waren,
Sie zwingt jetzt deines Szepters Macht.
Doch einer lebt noch, sie zu rächen,
Dich kann mein Mund nicht glücklich sprechen,
Solang des Feindes Auge wacht.«

Und eh der König noch geendet,
Da stellt sich, von Milet gesendet,
Ein Bote dem Tyrannen dar;
»Laß, Herr! des Opfers Düfte steigen
Und mit des Lorbeers muntern Zweigen
Bekränze dir dein festlich Haar.

Getroffen sank dein Feind vom Speere,
Mich sendet mit der frohen Märe
Dein treuer Feldherr Polydor—«
Und nimmt aus einem schwarzen Becken,
Noch blutig, zu der beiden Schrecken,
Ein wohlbekanntes Haupt hervor.

Der König tritt zurück mit Grauen:
»Doch warn ich dich, dem Glück zu trauen«,
Versetzt er mit besorgtem Blick.
»Bedenk, auf ungetreuen Wellen,
Wie leicht kann sie der Sturm zerschellen,
Schwimmt deiner Flotte zweifelnd Glück.«

Polycrates and His Ring

He stood upon his palace-wall.
His proud eye wandered over all
The wealth of Samos, east and west.
   "See! this is mine—all this *I* govern!"
  He said, addressing Egypt's Sovereign,
"Confess! my lot indeed is blest!"

"Yes, thou hast won the Gods' high favor,
For nobler men than thou, and braver,
Thy rivals once, are now thy slaves;
   But, Fate will soon revenge the wrong—
  I dare not call thee blest, so long
As Heaven is just or Earth has graves!"

While yet he spake, behold! there came
A messenger in Milo's name—
"Health to the great Polycrates!
   O King, braid laurels in thy hair,
  And let new Pæans thrill the air,
And incense-offerings load the breeze!

"Spear-pierced, thy rebel foe lies dead,
Behold! I bear the traitor's head,
Sent by thy General, Polydore."—
   Unrolling a dark shroud of cloth,
  He bared, before the gaze of both,
A ghastly head, still dropping gore!

The Stranger King shrank back a pace,
Then said—"Thou art of mortal race:
On earth Success but heralds Ill.
   Thou hast a fleet at sea: Beware!
  For waves and winds heed no man's prayer
And Tempest wakes at Neptune's will!"

Und eh er noch das Wort gesprochen,
Hat ihn der Jubel unterbrochen,
Der von der Reede jauchzend schallt.
Mit fremden Schätzen reich beladen,
Kehrt zu den heimischen Gestaden
Der Schiffe mastenreicher Wald.

Der königliche Gast erstaunet:
»Dein Glück ist heute gut gelaunet,
Doch fürchte seinen Unbestand.
Der Kreter waffenkundge Scharen
Bedräuen dich mit Kriegsgefahren,
Schon nahe sind sie diesem Strand.«

Und eh ihm noch das Wort entfallen,
Da sieht mans von den Schiffen wallen,
Und tausend Stimmen rufen ; »Sieg!
Von Feindesnot sind wir befreiet,
Die Kreter hat der Sturm zerstreuet,
Vorbei, geendet ist der Krieg.«

Das hört der Gastfreund mit Entsetzen:
»Fürwahr, ich muß dich glücklich schätzen,
Doch«, spricht er, »zittr ich für dein Heil.
Mir grauet vor der Götter Neide,
Des Lebens ungemischte Freude
Ward keinem Irdischen zuteil.

Auch mir ist alles wohlgeraten,
Bei allen meinen Herrschertaten
Begleitet mich des Himmels Huld,
Doch hatt ich einen teuren Erben,
Den nahm mir Gott, ich sah ihn sterben,
Dem Glück bezahlt' ich meine Schuld.

Drum, willst du dich vor Leid bewahren,
So flehe zu den Unsichtbaren,
Daß sie zum Glück den Schmerz verleihn.

But hark! a loud, a deafening shout
Of welcome from the throng without!
"Joy! joy!" The fleet so long away,
  So long away, so long awaited,
  At last is come, and, richly freighted,
Casts anchor in the exulting bay!"

The Royal Guest hears all, astounded.
"Thy triumphs, truly, *seem* unbounded,
But *are* they? No! Thy star will set;
  The javelins of the Cretan hordes
  Strike surer home than Samian swords,
And thou must fall before them yet!"—

Even while he warns again rejoice
The crowd with one tumultuous voice—
"Hurrah! Dread Sovereign, live alway!
  The war is over! Lo! the storms
  Have wrecked thy foes! The savage swarms
Of Crete and Thrace are Neptune's prey!"

"It is enough!" exclaimed the Guest:
Blind Mortal! call thyself The Blest—
Feel all that Pride and Conquest can!
  I here predict thine overthrow,
  For, perfect bliss, unstarred with woe,
Came never yet from God to Man.

"I too have been most fortunate:
At home, abroad, in camp and state,
The bounteous Gods long favored me—
  Yet I have wept! My only-cherished,
  My son died in my arms! He perished,
And paid my debt to Destiny.

"If thou, then, wilt propitiate Fate,
Pray God forthwith to adulterate
Thy Cup of Joy! In all my past

Noch keinen sah ich fröhlich enden,
Auf den mit immer vollen Händen
Die Götter ihre Gaben streun.

Und wenns die Götter nicht gewähren,
So acht auf eines Freundes Lehren
Und rufe selbst das Unglück her,
Und was von allen deinen Schätzen
Dein Herz am höchsten mag ergötzen,
Das nimm und wirfs in dieses Meer.«

Und jener spricht, von Furcht beweget:
»Von allem, was die Insel heget,
Ist dieser Ring mein höchstes Gut.
Ihn will ich den Erinnen weihen,
Ob sie mein Glück mir dann verzeihen.«
Und wirft das Kleinod in die Flut.

Und bei des nächsten Morgens Lichte,
Da tritt mit fröhlichem Gesichte
Ein Fischer vor den Fürsten hin:
»Herr, diesen Fisch hab ich gefangen,
Wie keiner noch ins Netz gegangen,
Dir zum Geschenke bring ich ihn.«

Und als der Koch den Fisch zerteilet,
Kommt er bestürzt herbeigeeilet
Und ruft mit hocherstauntem Blick:
»Sieh, Herr, den Ring, den du getragen,
Ihn fand ich in des Fisches Magen,
O, ohne Grenzen ist dein Glück!«

Hier wendet sich der Gast mit Grausen:
»So kann ich hier nicht ferner hausen,
Mein Freund kannst du nicht weiter sein.
Die Götter wollen dein Verderben,
Fort eil ich, nicht mit dir zu sterben.«
Und sprachs und schiffte schnell sich ein.

Experience never knew I one
Who too long filled a golden throne,
But Ruin crushed the wretch at last!

"But if God will not hear thy prayer,
Then woo Misfortune by some snare,
Even as the fowler sets his gin.
   Hast here some jewel, some rare treasure,
   Thou lovest, prizest beyond measure?
The sea rolls yonder—hurl it in!"

Replied the Host, now seized with fear,
"My realm hath naught I hold so dear
As this resplendent opal ring;
   If *that* may calm the Furies' wrath,
   Behold! I cast it in their path;"—
And forth he flung the glittering thing.

But when the morn again was come,
There stood without the palace-dome
A fisher with his teeming flasket,
   Who cried, "Great King, thy days be pleasant.
   Thou wilt not scorn my humble present,
This fish, the choicest in my basket."

And ere the mid-day meal the cook,
With joy and wonder in his look,
Rushed in, and fell before his Master—
   "O glorious Victor! matchless King!
   Within the fish I found thy ring!
Thou wast not born to know Disaster!"

Hereon uprose the Guest in dread:
"I tarry here too long," he said;
"O prosperous wretch! my *friend* no more!
   The Gods have willed thy swift perdition!
   I will not bide the Avenger's mission!"
He spake, and straightway left the shore.

James Clarence Mangan

Das Glück

Selig, welchen die Götter, die gnädigen, vor der Geburt schon
    Liebten, welchen als Kind Venus im Arme gewiegt,
Welchem Phöbus die Augen, die Lippen Hermes gelöset
    Und das Siegel der Macht Zeus auf die Stirne gedrückt!
Ein erhabenes Los, ein göttliches, ist ihm gefallen,
    Schon vor des Kampfes Beginn sind ihm die Schläfen bekränzt.
Ihm ist, eh er es lebte, das volle Leben gerechnet,
    Eh er die Mühe bestand, hat er die Charis erlangt.

Groß zwar nenn' ich den Mann, der, sein eigner Bildner und
    Schöpfer,
    Durch der Tugend Gewalt selber die Parze bezwingt;
Aber nicht erzwingt er das Glück, und was ihm die Charis
    Neidisch geweigert, erringt nimmer der strebende Mut.
Vor Unwürdigem kann dich der Wille, der ernste, bewahren,
    Alles Höchste, es kommt frei von den Göttern herab.
Wie die Geliebte dich liebt, so kommen die himmlischen Gaben;
    Oben in Jupiters Reich herrscht, wie in Amors, die Gunst.
Neigungen haben die Götter, sie lieben der grünenden Jugend
    Lockigte Scheitel, es zieht Freude die Fröhlichen an.
Nicht der Sehende wird von ihrer Erscheinung beseligt,
    Ihrer Herrlichkeit Glanz hat nur der Blinde geschaut.
Gern erwählen sie sich der Einfalt kindliche Seele,
    In das bescheidne Gefäß schließen sie Göttliches ein.
Ungehofft sind sie da und täuschen die stolze Erwartung,
    Keines Bannes Gewalt zwinget die Freien herab.
Wem er geneigt, dem sendet der Vater der Menschen und Götter
    Seinen Adler herab, trägt ihn zu himmlischen Höhn.
Unter die Menge greift er mit Eigenwillen, und welches
    Haupt ihm gefället, um das flicht er mit liebender Hand
Jetzt den Lorbeer und jetzt die herrschaftgebende Binde,
    Krönte doch selber den Gott nur das gewogene Glück.

The Gifts of Fortune

Blessed whom, ere he was born, the gods for their favors had
    chosen,
    Whom, while he was but a child, Venus held up in her arms.
Phoebus opens his eyes, his lips are untied by Hermes,
    And the emblem of might Zeus imprints on his brow.
Truly, sublime is his prospect. The fate that befell him is godlike.
    His is the victor's crown long ere the fray has begun;
Long ere he starts on his journey, its goal is reckoned
    accomplished;
    Ere he has proven his worth, safe he stands sheltered in grace.

Great, to be sure, will I call the other who—self-made and
    self-trained—
    Alters, by virtue's strength, even the Moira's decree.
Never the gifts of Fortune will thus be compelled. What is given
    Only by grace must remain outside the pale of man's will.
Earnest endeavor can help one to vanquish the powers of evil,
    But the ultimate good unbidden descends from on high.
Heaven bestows its gifts as love is bestowed by lovers:
    Favor rules Cupid's realm, likewise the realm of Zeus.
Think not the gods impartial. The curls of youth may bewitch them.
    Gay in their hearts themselves, fain with the gay they consort.
Not the keen-eyed observer is granted the bliss to behold them;
    Only the unknowing blind witness their splendorous light.
Often they choose for their gifts the simple soul of the childlike,
    Casting in humblest forms substance of heavenly kin.
Coming where least awaited, they foil him who proudly expects
    them:
    There is no magic, no spell potent to cast them in bonds.
Whom the Father of men and Immortals has chosen his minion
    He bids his eagle seek out, carry to heavenly heights.
Guided by whim or fancy, the god finds the one among many
    Whom he decides to like, and with a loving hand
Crowns with laurels or fillet of power the head he has chosen,
    For he himself wears his crown only by Fortune's grace.

Vor dem Glücklichen her tritt Phöbus, der pythische Sieger,
    Und, der die Herzen bezwingt, Amor, der lächelnde Gott.
Vor ihm ebnet Poseidon das Meer, sanft gleitet des Schiffes
    Kiel, das den Cäsar führt und sein allmächtiges Glück.
Ihm zu Füßen legt sich der Leu, das brausende Delphin
    Steigt aus den Tiefen, und fromm beut es den Rücken ihm an.

Zürne dem Glücklichen nicht, daß den leichten Sieg ihm die
       Götter
    Schenken, daß aus der Schlacht Venus den Liebling entrückt.
Ihn, den die Lächelnde rettet, den Göttergeliebten beneid' ich,
    Jenen nicht, dem sie mit Nacht deckt den verdunkelten Blick.
War er weniger herrlich, Achilles, weil ihm Hephästos
    Selbst geschmiedet den Schild und das verderbliche Schwert?
Weil um den sterblichen Mann der große Olymp sich beweget?
    Das verherrlichet ihn, daß ihn die Götter geliebt,
Daß sie sein Zürnen geehrt und, Ruhm dem Liebling zu geben,
    Hellas' bestes Geschlecht stürzten zum Orkus hinab.
Zürne der Schönheit nicht, daß sie schön ist, daß sie verdienstlos,
    Wie der Lilie Kelch prangt durch der Venus Geschenk!
Laß sie die Glückliche sein; du schaust sie, du bist der Beglückte!
    Wie sie ohne Verdienst glänzt, so entzücket sie dich.
Freue dich, daß die Gabe des Lieds vom Himmel herabkommt,
    Daß der Sänger dir singt, was ihn die Muse gelehrt:
Weil der Gott ihn beseelt, so wird er dem Hörer zum Gotte;
    Weil er der Glückliche ist, kannst du der Selige sein.
Auf dem geschäftigen Markt, da führe Themis die Waage,
    Und es messe der Lohn streng an der Mühe sich ab;
Aber die Freude ruft nur ein Gott auf sterbliche Wangen,
    Wo kein Wunder geschieht, ist kein Beglückter zu sehn.

Alles Menschliche muß erst werden und wachsen und reifen,
    Und von Gestalt zu Gestalt führt es die bildende Zeit;
Aber das Glückliche siehest du nicht, das Schöne nicht werden,
    Fertig von Ewigkeit her steht es vollendet vor dir.

Smoothed is the path of the fortunate mortal by Phoebus Apollo
  And that subduer of hearts, Amor, the smiling god.
Neptune quiets the ocean before him, and blithely his vessel—
  "Caesar aboard and his luck"—follows his charted course.
Gently the lion lies down at his feet, and the agile dolphin
  Pushes its back into view, ready to serve as his mount.

Do not resent that the gods grant the favored few effortless triumphs
  Or that whom Venus prefers safely she whisks from the fight.
Worthy of praise deems the world whom the smiling goddess has
  rescued,
  Paying the other no heed whom she let sink to the shades.
Do we account Achilles' glory impaired since Hephaestus
  Fashioned his mighty shield and his destructive sword,
Since for this one mortal human all of Olympus is stirring?
  No, it glorifies him that he is loved by the gods,
That they would honor his wrath, and, for the sake of his glory,
  Plunge the flower of Greece into the Hadean night.
Do not resent that beauty's beauty stems from no merit,
  That it is Venus's gift, free as the blossoms of Spring.
Let beauty enjoy its good fortune. Behold it and share the
  enjoyment.
  Undeserved are its charms. So is your power to see.
Let us rejoice that the gift of song has descended from heaven,
  That the poet, for us, sings what he learned from the Muse.
Holding his fief from a god, he appears as a god to us hearers,
  Being by Fortune endowed, bliss he reflects upon us.
In the affairs of the market let Themis hold sway with her balance.
  There the weight of the toil measures by rights the reward.
Not so with joy. It appears when a god has decreed its
  appearance:
  Only a miracle can conjure its warmth to men's hearts.

Everything human must slowly arise, must unfold, and must ripen:
  Ever from phase to phase plastic time leads it on.
But neither beauty nor fortune are ever born into being:
  Perfect ere time began, perfect they face us today.

Jede irdische Venus ersteht, wie die erste des Himmels,
  Eine dunkle Geburt, aus dem unendlichen Meer;
Wie die erste Minerva, so tritt, mit der Ägis gerüstet,
  Aus des Donnerers Haupt jeder Gedanke des Lichts.

Nänie

Auch das Schöne muß sterben! Das Menschen und Götter
    bezwinget,
  Nicht die eherne Brust rührt es des stygischen Zeus.
Einmal nur erweichte die Liebe den Schattenbeherrscher,
  Und an der Schwelle noch, streng, rief er zurück sein Geschenk.
Nicht stillt Aphrodite dem schönen Knaben die Wunde,
  Die in den zierlichen Leib grausam der Eber geritzt.
Nicht errettet den göttlichen Held die unsterbliche Mutter,
  Wann er, am skäischen Tor fallend, sein Schicksal erfüllt.
Aber sie steigt aus dem Meer mit allen Töchtern des Nereus,
  Und die Klage hebt an um den verherrlichten Sohn.
Siehe! Da weinen die Götter, es weinen die Göttinnen alle,
  Daß das Schöne vergeht, daß das Vollkommene stirbt.
Auch ein Klaglied zu sein im Mund der Geliebten, ist herrlich,
  Denn das Gemeine geht klanglos zum Orkus hinab.

Johann Gaudenz von Salis-Seewis

Lied, zu singen bei einer Wasserfahrt

Wir ruhen, vom Wasser gewiegt,
Im Kreise vertraulich und enge;
Durch Eintracht wie Blumengehänge

Every Venus on earth emerges, as did the divine one,
    As an occult event from the infinite sea.
Perfect, like the divine Minerva, equipped with the aegis,
    So every light-bearing thought springs from the Thunderer's head.

Alexander Gode

Nenia

Also the beautiful dies.—Its spell binds all men and immortals
    Save one: the Stygian Zeus. Armored in steel is his breast.
Once only did soften a lover the ruler of Hades.
    Yet, ere the threshold was reached, sternly he canceled his gift.
As Aphrodite stills not the gaping wounds of Adonis
    Which on the beautiful youth, hunted, the wild boar inflicts,
So the immortal Thetis saves not her divine son Achilles
    When at the Scaean Gate, falling, he meets with his fate.
But from the sea she arises with all the daughters of Nereus,
    And they intone their lament for her transfigured son.
Lo, all the gods now are weeping and weeping is every goddess
    That the beautiful wanes, that the perfect must die.
Glory is also to be a song of sorrow of loved ones,
    For, what is vulgar goes down songless to echoless depths.

Alexander Gode

Johann Gaudenz von Salis-Seewis

Song to be Sung During a Trip on the Water

Water-cradled, we rest as we go,
Cozy our circle and small,
In harmony wreathed like the fall

Verknüpft und in Reihen gefügt;
Uns sondert von lästiger Menge
Die Flut, die den Nachen umschmiegt.

So gleiten, im Raume vereint,
Wir auf der Vergänglichkeit Wellen,
Wo Freunde sich innig gesellen
Zum Freunde, der redlich es meint,
Getrost, weil die dunkelsten Stellen
Ein Glanz aus der Höhe bescheint.

Ach trüg' uns die fährliche Flut
Des Lebens so friedlich und leise!
O drohte nie Trennung dem Kreise,
Der sorglos um Zukunft hier ruht!
O nähm' uns am Ziele der Reise
Elysiums Busen in Hut!

Verhallen mag unser Gesang
Wie Flötenhauch schwinden das Leben;
Mit Jubel und Seufzern verschweben
Des Daseins zerfließender Klang!
Der Geist wird verklärt sich erheben,
Wann Lethe sein Fahrzeug verschlang.

Friedrich Hölderlin

Hyperions Schicksalslied

Ihr wandelt droben im Licht
   Auf weichem Boden, selige Genien!
     Glänzende Götterlüfte
      Rühren euch leicht,
        Wie die Finger der Künstlerin
        Heilige Saiten.

Of garlands hung row upon row,
Borne away from the crowd's madding call
By our boat and the river's soft flow.

So, joined in the world, we shall glide
On time's swiftly vanishing stream,
And, bonded by honest esteem,
We friends in sure friendship abide,
Secure, since a heaven-sent gleam
Spreads its light where dark's darknesses hide.

Oh, would that life's dangerous crest
Bore us ever thus, gently and still,
Oh, would that the threat of farewell
Never shadowed us, carefree and blest,
Oh would, journey ended, the swell
Bring us safe to Elysium's breast.

Echoes die, and the notes of our song,
Like the breath of the flute our life flies,
Amid joyful sounds and with sighs
Our being's tune fails and is done.
Transfigured, the spirit will rise,
When its vessel to Lethe has gone.

G. C. Schoolfield

Friedrich Hölderlin

Hyperion's Song of Fate

You walk up there in the light
    On floors like velvet, blissful spirits.
        Shining winds divine
            Touch you lightly
                As a harper touches holy
                    Strings with her fingers.

Schicksallos, wie der schlafende
Säugling, atmen die Himmlischen;
Keusch bewahrt
In bescheidener Knospe,
Blühet ewig
Ihnen der Geist,
Und die seligen Augen
Blicken in stiller
Ewiger Klarheit.

Doch uns ist gegeben,
Auf keiner Stätte zu ruhn,
Es schwinden, es fallen
Die leidenden Menschen
Blindlings von einer
Stunde zur andern,
Wie Wasser von Klippe
Zu Klippe geworfen,
Jahr lang ins Ungewisse hinab.

Abendphantasie

Vor seiner Hütte ruhig im Schatten sitzt
Der Pflüger, dem Genügsamen raucht sein Herd.
Gastfreundlich tönt dem Wanderer im
Friedlichen Dorfe die Abendglocke.

Wohl kehren itzt die Schiffer zum Hafen auch,
In fernen Städten, fröhlich verrauscht des Markts
Geschäftger Lärm; in stiller Laube
Glänzt das gesellige Mahl den Freunden.

Wohin denn ich? Es leben die Sterblichen
Von Lohn und Arbeit; wechselnd in Müh und Ruh
Ist alles freudig; warum schläft denn
Nimmer nur mir in der Brust der Stachel?

Fateless as babes asleep
They breathe, the celestials.
Chastely kept
In a simple bud,
For them the spirit
Flowers eternal,
And in bliss their eyes
Gaze in eternal
Calm clarity.

But to us it is given
To find no resting place,
We faint, we fall,
Suffering, human,
Blindly from one
To the next moment
Like water flung
From rock to rock down
Long years into uncertainty.

Christopher Middleton

Evening Fantasy

Before his shaded threshold the plowman sits,
Contented; smoke ascends from the warming hearth.
A welcome rings to wanderers from
Evening bells in the peaceful village.

The sailors must be coming to port now, too,
In distant cities; gaily the market's noise
Recedes, is still; in quiet arbors
Friends take their meals in convivial splendor.

And where am *I* to go? Other mortals live
From pay and labor, alternate work and rest,
And all is joyful; why does only
My heart not rest, with its constant stinging?

Am Abendhimmel blühet ein Frühling auf;
  Unzählig blühn die Rosen und ruhig scheint
    Die goldne Welt; o dorthin nimmt mich,
      Purpurne Wolken! und möge droben

In Licht und Luft zerrinnen mir Lieb und Leid!—
  Doch, wie verscheucht von töriger Bitte, flieht
    Der Zauber; dunkel wirds und einsam
      Unter dem Himmel, wie immer, bin ich—

Komm du nun, sanfter Schlummer! zu viel begehrt
  Das Herz; doch endlich, Jugend! verglühst du ja,
    Du ruhelose, träumerische!
      Friedlich und heiter ist dann das Alter.

Menschenbeifall

Ist nicht heilig mein Herz, schöneren Lebens voll,
  Seit ich liebe? warum achtetet ihr mich mehr,
    Da ich stolzer und wilder,
      Wortereicher und leerer war?

Ach! der Menge gefällt, was auf den Marktplatz taugt,
  Und es ehret der Knecht nur den Gewaltsamen;
    An das Göttliche glauben
      Die allein, die es selber sind.

An die jungen Dichter

Lieben Brüder! es reift unsere Kunst vielleicht,
  Da, dem Jünglinge gleich, lange sie schon gegärt,
    Bald zur Stille der Schönheit;
      Seid nur fromm, wie der Grieche war!

A spring-like garden blooms in the evening sky,
   The countless roses blossom, and peaceful seems
      The golden world; O take me with you,
         Lavender clouds, and up there then may in

The light and air my bliss and my grief dissolve!—
   But as if frightened off by my foolish plea,
      The spell is gone; it's dark; and lonely
         Under the heavens I stand, as always.

So come to me, soft slumber; my heart has wished
   Too much; but someday, youth, you will lose your glow,
      You restless youth, forever dreaming.
         Peaceful and cheerful are then the aged.

                    Kenneth Negus

Public Approval

Has my heart not become sacred and filled with life
   Since I've loved? Why did they grant me so much respect,
      When my pride and my wildness
         Made me wordy and emptier?

Yes, the masses prefer merely what money buys
   And the vassal respects only a show of force;
      Only those who are godly,
         In themselves, honor godliness.

                    Kenneth Negus

To Young Poets

Friends and brothers, our art soon perhaps will mature,
   Soon will grow (like a youth, long-fermenting) and then
      Rise in stillness of beauty;
         Just be pious, as Grecians were.

Liebt die Götter und denkt freundlich der Sterblichen!
Haßt den Rausch, wie den Frost! lehrt, und beschreibet nicht!
    Wenn der Meister euch ängstigt,
        Fragt die große Natur um Rat.

An die Parzen

Nur Einen Sommer gönnt, ihr Gewaltigen!
Und einen Herbst zu reifem Gesange mir,
    Daß williger mein Herz, vom süßen
        Spiele gesättiget, dann mir sterbe.

Die Seele, der im Leben ihr göttlich Recht
    Nicht ward, sie ruht auch drunten im Orkus nicht;
        Doch ist mir einst das Heilge, das am
            Herzen mir liegt, das Gedicht, gelungen,

Willkommen dann, o Stille der Schattenwelt!
    Zufrieden bin ich, wenn auch mein Saitenspiel
        Mich nicht hinab geleitet; Einmal
            Lebt ich, wie Götter, und mehr bedarf's nicht.

Diotima

Du schweigst und duldest, und sie verstehn dich nicht,
    Du heilig Leben! welkest hinweg und schweigst,
        Denn ach, vergebens bei Barbaren
            Suchst du die Deinen im Sonnenlichte,

Die zärtlichgroßen Seelen, die nimmer sind!
    Doch eilt die Zeit. Noch siehet mein sterblich Lied
        Den Tag, der, Diotima! nächst den
            Göttern mit Helden dich nennt, und dir gleicht.

Love the gods, be disposed kindly toward all men;
  Be not drunken, nor cold; neither teach nor describe.
    If the master then scolds you,
      Ask great Nature for her advice.

Kenneth Negus

To the Fates

One summer only grant me, you powerful Fates,
  And one more autumn only for mellow song,
    So that more willingly, replete with
      Music's late sweetness, my heart may die then.

The soul in life denied its god-given right
  Down there in Orcus also will find no peace;
    But when what's holy, dear to me, the
      Poem's accomplished, my art perfected,

Then welcome, silence, welcome cold world of shades!
  I'll be content, though here I must leave my lyre
    And songless travel down; for *once* I
      Lived like the gods, and no more is needed.

Michael Hamburger

Diotima

You suffer and keep silent and, strange to them,
  You holy being, silently wilt away;
    For, ah, in vain among barbarians
      Here in the sunlight you seek your kindred,

The nobly tender spirits that are no more!
  Yet time speeds on. Though mortal, my song will live
    To see the day which next to gods, with
      Heroes will name you, itself be like you.

Michael Hamburger

Geh unter, schöne Sonne . . .

Geh unter, schöne Sonne, sie achteten
Nur wenig dein, sie kannten dich, Heil'ge, nicht,
    Denn mühelos und stille bist du
      Über den mühsamen aufgegangen.

Mir gehst du freundlich unter und auf, o Licht!
Und wohl erkennt mein Auge dich, herrliches!
    Denn göttlich stille ehren lernt ich,
      Da Diotima den Sinn mir heilte.

O du, des Himmels Botin! wie lauscht ich dir!
Dir, Diotima! Liebe! wie sah von dir
    Zum goldnen Tage dieses Auge
      Glänzend und dankbar empor. Da rauschten

Lebendiger die Quellen, es atmeten
Der dunkeln Erde Blüten mich liebend an,
    Und lächelnd über Silberwolken
      Neigte sich segnend herab der Äther.

Der Abschied

Zweite Fassung

Trennen wollten wir uns? wähnten es gut und klug?
    Da wirs taten, warum schröckte, wie Mord, die Tat?
      Ach! wir kennen uns wenig,
        Denn es waltet ein Gott in uns.

Den verraten? ach ihn, welcher uns alles erst,
    Sinn und Leben erschuf, ihn, den beseelenden
      Schutzgott unserer Liebe,
        Dies, dies Eine vermag ich nicht.

Go down, fair sun . . .

Go down, fair sun, unnoticed by nearly all
The race of men, your sanctity unperceived,
   Because untoiling you have soared and
     Silently risen above the toiling.

To me you rise and set as a friend, O light,
Your splendour is familiar to my eye
   Since Diotima healed my soul and
     Taught me to worship in holy silence.

O envoy sent from heaven, your every word
I drank upon your lips, Diotima! Love!
   To golden days from you I lifted
     Grateful and marvelling eyes. Behold then,

The bubbling springs were fuller of life, the blooms
Caressed me with their breath on the darkling earth,
   And smiling from his throne in clouds of
     Silver the Aether bent down to bless us.

Elizabeth Henderson

The Farewell

Second Version

Did we intend to part, thinking it good and wise?
   Why did the act once done shock us like murder? Ah,
     Little we understand
       Ourselves, for a god is in us.

Fail him? Ah, fail the one who for us created
   All meaning and all life, into our love
     Put life and soul, guarding it,
       This one thing I cannot do.

Aber anderen Fehl denket der Weltsinn sich,
  Andern ehernen Dienst übt er und anders Recht,
    Und es listet die Seele
      Tag für Tag der Gebrauch uns ab.

Wohl! ich wußt es zuvor. Seit die gewurzelte
  Ungestalte, die Furcht Götter und Menschen trennt,
    Muß, mit Blut sie zu sühnen,
      Muß der Liebenden Herz vergehn.

Laß mich schweigen! o laß nimmer von nun an mich
  Dieses Tödliche sehn, daß ich im Frieden doch
    Hin ins Einsame ziehe,
      Und noch unser der Abschied sei!

Reich die Schale mir selbst, daß ich des rettenden
  Heilgen Giftes genug, daß ich des Lethetranks
    Mit dir trinke, daß alles,
      Haß und Liebe, vergessen sei!

Hingehn will ich. Vielleicht seh ich in langer Zeit
  Diotima! dich hier. Aber verblutet ist
    Dann das Wünschen und friedlich
      Gleich den Seligen, fremde gehn

Wir umher, ein Gespräch führet uns ab und auf,
  Sinnend, zögernd, doch itzt mahnt die Vergessenen
    Hier die Stelle des Abschieds,
      Es erwarmet ein Herz in uns,

Staunend seh ich dich an, Stimmen und süßen Sang,
  Wie aus voriger Zeit, hör ich und Saitenspiel,
    Und die Lilie duftet
      Golden über dem Bach uns auf.

But meaning a different fault the world's intent
   Practises a different task, hard, different laws;
     Custom and habit snaffle
       Day by day the soul from us.

So be it. I knew as much. Since ever rooted
   Malformity, fear, cleft gods and men apart,
     Must with blood to atone them
       Mortal hearts in love pass on.

Do not have me speak, let me never again behold
   This deadly thing, that I may make my way in peace,
     At least, into solitude,
       And let this parting be our own.

Hand me the cup yourself, that I with you may drink
   The holy bane, enough, the saving draft, and drink
     Lethe's oblivion, that we may both
       Forget the hate and the love also.

I go, willing. Long hence, perhaps, Diotima, I
   Shall see you here. But wishes will have bled away,
     And all at peace, like souls
       Of the departed, we shall walk about,

Strangers, conversation leading us up and down,
   Pensive, hesitant, though now the place of our farewell
     Reminds us, who shall be forgotten,
       A heart grows warm in us,

I look at you with wonder, voices I hear and sweet
   Song as from a time gone by, and music of strings,
     And the lily wafts to us,
       Golden, its fragrance above the stream.

Christopher Middleton

Andenken

Der Nordost wehet,
Der liebste unter den Winden
Mir, weil er feurigen Geist
Und gute Fahrt verheißet den Schiffern.
Geh aber nun und grüße
Die schöne Garonne,
Und die Gärten von Bourdeaux
Dort, wo am scharfen Ufer
Hingehet der Steg und in den Strom
Tief fällt der Bach, darüber aber
Hinschauet ein edel Paar
Von Eichen und Silberpappeln;

Noch denket das mir wohl und wie
Die breiten Gipfel neiget
Der Ulmwald, über die Mühl,
Im Hofe aber wächset ein Feigenbaum.
An Feiertagen gehn
Die braunen Frauen daselbst
Auf seidnen Boden,
Zur Märzenzeit,
Wenn gleich ist Nacht und Tag,
Und über langsamen Stegen,
Von goldenen Träumen schwer,
Einwiegende Lüfte ziehen.

Es reiche aber,
Des dunkeln Lichtes voll,
Mir einer den duftenden Becher,
Damit ich ruhen möge; denn süß
Wär unter Schatten der Schlummer.
Nicht ist es gut,
Seellos von sterblichen
Gedanken zu sein. Doch gut
Ist ein Gespräch und zu sagen

Remembrance

The northeaster blows,
Best loved of all the winds
For me, as it promises
Fiery spirit and a good voyage
For seafarers. But now go and greet
The beautiful Garonne
And the gardens of Bordeaux,
Where on the steep
Riverbank the path slopes
Down and the stream
Falls into it, sheer, but
A noble pair of oaks upstands,
And silver poplars, gazing.

Thoughts of this are pleasant still, and how
The wide treetops of the elmwood
Bow across the mill,
But a figtree grows in the courtyard.
There on holidays
Brown women walk
On silken ground,
When March is come
And day and night are equal,
And over slow footpaths
Weighted with golden dreams
The lulling breezes move.

But hand me,
Someone, the fragrant cup
Brimming with dark light, that I
May rest; sleep
Would be sweet, in the shadows.
It is not good
To let mortal thoughts
Empty the soul. But conversation
Is good, and to say

Des Herzens Meinung, zu hören viel
Von Tagen der Lieb,
Und Taten, welche geschehen.

Wo aber sind die Freunde? Bellarmin
Mit dem Gefährten? Mancher
Trägt Scheue, an die Quelle zu gehn;
Es beginnet nämlich der Reichtum
Im Meere. Sie,
Wie Maler, bringen zusammen
Das Schöne der Erd und verschmähn
Den geflügelten Krieg nicht, und
Zu wohnen einsam, jahrlang, unter
Dem entlaubten Mast, wo nicht die Nacht durchglänzen
Die Feiertage der Stadt,
Und Saitenspiel und eingeborener Tanz nicht.

Nun aber sind zu Indiern
Die Männer gegangen,
Dort an der luftigen Spitz
An Traubenbergen, wo herab
Die Dordogne kommt,
Und zusammen mit der prächtgen
Garonne meerbreit
Ausgehet der Strom. Es nehmet aber
Und gibt Gedächtnis die See,
Und die Lieb auch heftet fleißig die Augen,
Was bleibet aber, stiften die Dichter.

Lebensalter

Ihr Städte des Euphrats!
Ihr Gassen von Palmyra!
Ihr Säulenwälder in der Ebne der Wüste,
Was seid ihr?
Euch hat die Kronen,

What the heart means, to hear
Much about days of love
And deeds that have been done.

   But where are my friends, Bellarmin
With his companion? Some hesitate
To go to the source;
For in the sea
Plenitude does begin. They
Like painters compose
The beauty that is of earth, and do not shun
Winged war and to live
Years on end alone before the unleafed mast,
Where no town festivals
Make luminous the night,
Nor music, nor dancing of country folk.

   But now to the Indians
The men have gone,
There by the windy point,
By grape-clustering hills, down which
The Dordogne comes, and outward
With the glorious Garonne
Seawide the waters roll. But remembrance,
The sea takes it and gives it,
And love, too, intently steadies the gaze;
But poets alone ordain what abides.

Christopher Middleton

The Ages of Life

   You cities of Euphrates,
You streets at Palmyra,
You forests of pillars in the desert plain,
What are you?
Your crests, as you passed beyond

Dieweil ihr über die Grenze
Der Atmenden seid gegangen,
Von Himmlischen der Rauchdampf und
Hinweg das Feuer genommen;
Jetzt aber sitz ich unter Wolken (deren
Ein jedes eine Ruh' hat eigen) unter
Wohl eingerichteten Eichen, auf
Der Heide des Rehs, und fremd
Erscheinen und gestorben mir
Der Seligen Geister.

Hälfte des Lebens

Mit gelben Birnen hänget
Und voll mit wilden Rosen
Das Land in den See,
Ihr holden Schwäne,
Und trunken von Küssen
Tunkt ihr das Haupt
Ins heilignüchterne Wasser.

Weh mir, wo nehm ich, wenn
Es Winter ist, die Blumen, und wo
Den Sonnenschein
Und Schatten der Erde?
Die Mauern stehn
Sprachlos und kalt, im Winde
Klirren die Fahnen.

The bounds of those who breathe,
By smoke of heavenly powers and
By fire were taken away;
But now I sit beneath clouds (each one
With a quietness all of its own) beneath
A pleasing order of oak-trees, on
The heath where the roe-deer feed, and strange
To me, remote and dead seem
The souls of the blessèd.

Michael Hamburger

Half of Life

Filled with yellow pears
And with wild roses,
The landscape hangs in the lake,
O gentle swans;
And drunk with kisses
You dip your heads
In the sacred sober water.

Alas, whence shall I take,
When it is winter, flowers and
Whence sunshine
And shadows on the ground?
The walls stand
Dumb and cold, the weathercocks
Whirr in the wind.

Willard R. Trask and
Alexander Gode

Friedrich von Hardenberg
("Novalis")

Hymnen an die Nacht

I

Welcher Lebendige, Sinnbegabte liebt nicht vor allen Wundererscheinungen des verbreiteten Raums um ihn das allerfreuliche Licht—mit seinen Farben, seinen Strahlen und Wogen; seiner milden Allgegenwart, als weckender Tag. Wie des Lebens innerste Seele atmet es der rastlosen Gestirne Riesenwelt und schwimmt tanzend in seiner blauen Flut—atmet es der funkelnde, ewigruhende Stein, die sinnige, saugende Pflanze und das wilde, brennende, vielgestaltige Tier—vor allen aber der herrliche Fremdling mit den sinnvollen Augen, dem schwebenden Gange und den zartgeschlossenen, tonreichen Lippen. Wie ein König der irdischen Natur ruft es jede Kraft zu zahllosen Verwandlungen, knüpft und löst unendliche Bündnisse, hängt sein himmlisches Bild jedem irdischen Wesen um.—Seine Gegenwart allein offenbart die Wunderherrlichkeit der Reiche der Welt.

Abwärts wend ich mich zu der heiligen, unausprechlichen, geheimnisvollen Nacht. Fernab liegt die Welt—in eine tiefe Gruft versenkt—wüst und einsam ist ihre Stelle. In den Saiten der Brust weht tiefe Wehmut. In Tautropfen will ich hinuntersinken und mit der Asche mich vermischen.—Fernen der Erinnerung, Wünsche der Jugend, der Kindheit Träume, des ganzen langen Lebens kurze Freuden und vergebliche Hoffnungen kommen in grauen Kleidern wie Abendnebel nach der Sonne Untergang. In andern Räumen schlug die lustigen Gezelte das Licht auf. Sollte es nie zu seinen Kindern wiederkommen, die mit der Unschuld Glauben seiner harren?

Was quillt auf einmal so ahndungsvoll unterm Herzen und verschluckt der Wehmut weiche Luft? Hast auch du ein Gefallen an uns, dunkle Nacht? Was hältst du unter deinem Mantel, das mir unsichtbar kräftig an die Seele geht? Köstlicher Balsam träuft aus deiner Hand, aus dem Bündel Mohn. Die schweren Flügel des Ge-

Friedrich von Hardenberg ("Novalis")

Hymns to Night

I

What living being, sentiently endowed, does not love, above all the miraculous phenomena of space extending about it, all-rejoicing Light—with its colors, its beams and its waves; with its gentle omnipresence, as wakening day. The gigantic world of the restless stars breathes it as life's inmost soul, and swims, dancing, in its blue flood—the sparkling, eternally quiescent stone breathes it, the ingenious, nursing plant and the wild, burning, multiform beast—but above all the lordly stranger with thoughtful eyes, hovering gait, and tenderly closed, expressive lips. Like a king of earthly nature it summons every force to countless transformations, forms and dissolves endless alliances, hangs its heavenly image about every earthly being.—Its presence alone reveals the wondrous splendor of the realms of the world.

I turn aside to holy, ineffable, mysterious Night. Far away lies the world—sunk in a deep grave—deserted and lonely is its place. In the chords of my breast wafts deep nostalgia. In drops of dew let me sink down and mix with the ashes. Distant memories, youthful desires, dreams of childhood, all of long life's brief joys and vain hopes come in grey garments, like evening mists after sunset. In other regions Light has pitched its gay pavilions. Shall it never return to its children, who await it with the faith of innocence?

What suddenly wells up, so full of premonition, beneath my heart, absorbing nostalgia's gentle air? Do you too find pleasure in us, dark Night? What do you conceal beneath your cloak that presses upon my soul with invisible power? Precious balm drips from your hand, out of the bundle of poppies. You lift the heavy wings of heart and mind. Darkly and ineffably we feel ourselves moved—with a start of happy fright I see an earnest countenance softly and reverently inclined toward me, revealing beneath locks endlessly

müts hebst du empor. Dunkel und unaussprechlich fühlen wir uns
bewegt—ein ernstes Antilitz seh ich froh erschrocken, das sanft und
andachtsvoll sich zu mir neigt und unter unendlich verschlungenen
Locken der Mutter liebe Jugend zeigt. Wie arm und kindisch dünkt
mich das Licht nun—wie erfreulich und gesegnet des Tages Abschied.—Also nur darum, weil die Nacht dir abwendig macht die
Dienenden, säetest du in des Raumes Weiten die leuchtenden Ku-
geln, zu verkünden deine Allmacht—deine Wiederkehr—in den
Zeiten deiner Entfernung. Himmlischer als jene blitzenden Sterne
dünken uns die unendlichen Augen, die die Nacht in uns geöffnet.
Weiter sehn sie als die blässesten jener zahllosen Heere—unbe-
dürftig des Lichts, durchschaun sie die Tiefen eines liebenden Gemüts—was einen höhern Raum mit unsäglicher Wollust füllt. Preis
der Weltkönigin, der hohen Verkündigerin heiliger Welten, der
Pflegerin seliger Liebe—sie sendet mir dich—zarte Geliebte—liebliche Sonne der Nacht,—nun wach ich—denn ich bin dein und
mein—du hast die Nacht mir zum Leben verkündet—mich zum
Menschen gemacht—zehre mit Geisterglut meinen Leib, daß ich
luftig mit dir inniger mich mische und dann ewig die Brautnacht
währt.

II

Muß immer der Morgen wiederkommen? Endet nie des Irdischen
Gewalt? Unselige Geschäftigkeit verzehrt den himmlischen Anflug
der Nacht. Wird nie der Liebe geheimes Ofer ewig brennen? Zu-
gemessen ward dem Lichte seine Zeit; aber zeitlos und raumlos ist
der Nacht Herrschaft.—Ewig ist die Dauer des Schlafs. Heiliger
Schlaf—beglücke zu selten nicht der Nacht Geweihte in diesem irdischen Tagewerk. Nur die Toren verkennen dich und wissen von
keinem Schlafe als dem Schatten, den du in jener Dämmerung der
wahrhaften Nacht mitleidig auf uns wirfst. Sie fühlen dich nicht in
der goldenen Flut der Trauben—in des Mandelbaums Wunderöl
und dem braunen Safte des Mohns. Sie wissen nicht, daß du es
bist, der des zarten Mädchens Busen umschwebt und zum Himmel
den Schoß macht—ahnden nicht, daß aus alten Geschichten du
himmelöffnend entgegentrittst und den Schlüssel trägst zu den
Wohnungen der Seligen, unendlicher Geheimnisse schweigender
Bote.

entwined a Mother's dear youthfulness. How poor and childish Light seems to me now—how gratifying and blessed day's departure—So it was only because Night seduces your servants that you sowed those luminous orbs in the far reaches of space: to proclaim your omnipotence—your return—during the times of your absence. More heavenly than those blazing stars do we esteem the infinite eyes that Night has opened within us. They see farther than the palest of that innumerable host—without need of Light they see through the depths of a loving heart and mind—and that fills a higher space with unutterable delight. Praise to the World's Queen, the high heraldress of sacred worlds, to the nurse of blessed Love— she sends you to me—tender beloved—sweet Sun of Night,—now I wake—for I am thine and mine—you have made me human— have proclaimed Night to me as life—consume my body with spiritual fire, that, as air, I may commingle more inwardly with you and the wedding night then last forever.

II
Must morning always return? Will the might of the earthly never end? Accursed busy-ness consumes Night's heavenly touch. Will Love's secret sacrifice never burn forever? Light's days are measured; but timeless and spaceless is the reign of Night—Eternal is the duration of Sleep. Holy Sleep—bless not too seldom in their daily tasks those consecrated to Night. Only fools fail to recognize you and know no other sleep than the shadow you mercifully cast over us in that dusk of the true Night. They do not sense you in the grape's golden flood—in the almond tree's miraculous oil, in the brown juice of the poppy. They do not realize that it is you who hover about the bosom of the tender maiden and make a heaven of her womb—they have no inkling that it is you who comes to meet us in ancient tales, opening the heavens and bearing the keys to the dwellings of the blest, silent messenger of infinite mysteries.

III

Einst, da ich bittre Tränen vergoß, da in Schmerz aufgelöst meine Hoffnung zerrann und ich einsam stand am dürren Hügel, der in engem, dunkeln Raum die Gestalt meines Lebens barg—einsam, wie noch kein Einsamer war, von unsäglicher Angst getrieben—kraftlos, nur ein Gedanken des Elends noch,—wie ich da nach Hülfe umherschaute, vorwärts nicht konnte und rückwärts nicht und am fliehenden, verlöschten Leben mit unendlicher Sehnsucht hing:— da kam aus blauen Fernen—von den Höhen meiner alten Seligkeit ein Dämmerungsschauer—und mit einem Male riß das Band der Geburt—des Lichtes Fessel. Hin floh die irdische Herrlichkeit und meine Trauer mit ihr—zusammen floß die Wehmut in eine neue, unergründliche Welt—du, Nachtbegeisterung, Schlummer des Himmels, kamst über mich—die Gegend hob sich sacht empor; über der Gegend schwebte mein entbundner, neugeborner Geist. Zur Staubwolke wurde der Hügel—durch die Wolke sah ich die verklärten Züge der Geliebten. In Ihren Augen ruhte die Ewigkeit—ich faßte Ihre Hände, und die Tränen wurden ein funkelndes, unzerreißliches Band. Jahrtausende zogen abwärts in die Ferne, wie Ungewitter. An Ihrem Halse weint ich dem neuen Leben entzückende Tränen.—Es war der erste, einzige Traum—und erst seitdem fühl ich ewigen, unwandelbaren Glauben an den Himmel der Nacht und sein Licht, die Geliebte.

IV

Nun weiß ich, wenn der letzte Morgen sein wird—wenn das Licht nicht mehr die Nacht und die Liebe scheucht—wenn der Schlummer ewig und nur *ein* unerschöpflicher Traum sein wird. Himmlische Müdigkeit fühl ich in mir.—Weit und ermüdend ward mir die Wallfahrt zum heiligen Grabe, drückend das Kreuz. Die kristallene Woge, die, gemeinen Sinnen unvernehmlich, in des Hügels dunkelm Schoß quillt, an dessen Fuß die irdische Flut bricht, wer sie gekostet, wer oben stand auf dem Grenzgebürge der Welt, und hinübersah in das neue Land, in der Nacht Wohnsitz—wahrlich, der kehrt nicht in das Treiben der Welt zurück, in das Land, wo das Licht in ewiger Unruh hauset.

Oben baut er sich Hütten, Hütten des Friedens, sehnt sich und liebt, schaut hinüber, bis die willkommenste aller Stunden hinunter ihn in den Brunnen der Quelle zieht—das Irdische schwimmt

III

Once, as I wept bitter tears, as my hope, dissolved in pain, melted away, and I stood alone beside the barren mound that contained within its narrow, dark confines the form of my life—lonely, as no man has ever been, driven by unspeakable anguish—powerless, reduced to the essence of misery.—As I then cast about me for help, unable to go either forwards or backwards, but clinging to fleeting, extinguished life with infinite longing:—there came out of blue distances—from the heights of my former blessedness, a dusky thrill of awe—and, suddenly, the bond of birth broke—Light's fetter. Earthly splendor fled and my sadness with it—melancholy emptied into a new, unfathomable world—you, inspiration of Night, slumber of Heaven, came over me—the earth heaved gently; above it hovered my delivered, new-born spirit. The grave mound dissolved in a cloud of dust—through the cloud I beheld the transfigured features of my beloved. In Her eyes dwelt eternity—I took Her hands, my tears became a lucent, unbreakable bond. Millennia retreated into the distance, like thunderstorms. On Her neck I wept enraptured tears for the new life.—It was the first, the only, dream—and only since then do I feel eternal, inalterable belief in the heaven of Night and its Light, my beloved.

IV

Now I know when the last morning will come—when Light will no longer frighten away Night and Love—when slumber will be eternal and *one* inexhaustible dream. Heavenly weariness weighs within me.—Long and tiring was my pilgrimage to the Holy Sepulchre, oppressive the Cross. The crystal wave, imperceptible to ordinary senses, that wells up in the mound's dark womb, at whose foot breaks the earthly wave—he who has tasted of it, who has stood on the mountains that mark the limits of this world and gazed over into the new land, into the dwelling-place of Night—truly, he will not return to this world's busy-ness, to the land where Light dwells in eternal unrest.

On the heights he will build himself booths, booths of peace, will yearn and love, gazing over into that land until the most welcome of all hours draws him down into the well of the source—

obenauf, wird von Stürmen zurückgeführt, aber was heilig durch
der Liebe Berührung ward, rinnt aufgelöst in verborgenen Gängen
auf das jenseitige Gebiet, wo es, wie Düfte, sich mit entschlum-
merten Lieben mischt. Noch weckst du, muntres Licht, den Müden zur Arbeit—flößest fröhliches Leben mir ein—aber du lockst
mich von der Erinnerung moosigem Denkmal nicht. Gern will ich
die fleißigen Hände rühren, überall umschaun, wo du mich
brauchst—rühmen deines Glanzes volle Pracht—unverdrossen ver-
folgen deines künstlichen Werks schönen Zusammenhang—gern
betrachten deiner gewaltigen, leuchtenden Uhr sinnvollen Gang—
ergründen der Kräfte Ebenmaß und die Regeln des Wunderspiels
unzähliger Räume und ihrer Zeiten. Aber getreu der Nacht bleibt
mein geheimes Herz, und der schaffenden Liebe, ihrer Tochter.
Kannst du mir zeigen ein ewig treues Herz? Hat deine Sonne
freundliche Augen, die mich erkennen? Fassen deine Sterne meine
verlangende Hand? Geben mir wieder den zärtlichen Druck und
das kosende Wort? Hast du mit Farben und leichtem Umriß Sie
geziert—oder war Sie es, die deinem Schmuck höhere, liebere Be-
deutung gab? Welche Wollust, welchen Genuß bietet dein Leben,
die aufwögen des Todes Entzückungen? Trägt nicht alles, was uns
begeistert, die Farbe der Nacht? Sie trägt dich mütterlich, und ihr
verdankst du all deine Herrlichkeit. Du verflögst in dir selbst—in
endlosen Raum zergingst du, wenn sie dich nicht hielte, dich nicht
bände, daß du warm würdest und flammend die Welt zeugtest.
Wahrlich, ich war, eh du warst—die Mutter schickte mit meinen
Geschwistern mich, zu bewohnen deine Welt, sie zu heiligen mit
Liebe, daß sie ein ewig angeschautes Denkmal werde—zu bepflan-
zen sie mit unverwelklichen Blumen. Noch reiften sie nicht, diese
göttlichen Gedanken—Noch sind der Spuren unserer Offenbarung
wenig—Einst zeigt deine Uhr das Ende der Zeit, wenn du wirst wie
unsereiner und voll Sehnsucht und Inbrunst auslöschest und stirbst.
In mir fühl ich deiner Geschäftigkeit Ende—himmlische Freiheit,
selige Rückkehr. In wilden Schmerzen erkenn ich deine Entfernung
von unsrer Heimat, deinen Widerstand gegen den alten, herrlichen
Himmel. Deine Wut und dein Toben ist vergebens. Unverbrenn-
lich steht das Kreuz—eine Siegesfahne unsers Geschlechts.

> Hinüber wall ich,
> Und jede Pein

what is earthly floats on top and is carried back by storms, but what has been sanctified by the touch of Love flows, dissolved, in hidden channels to the region beyond, where it mingles, like vapors, with slumbering loved ones. Still do you awaken, vigorous Light, the weary one to his tasks—still do you infuse me with cheerful life—but from Memory's mossy monument you cannot tempt me. Willingly will I bestir myself, look about me everywhere to see where you may need me—praise your splendor's full glory— tirelessly trace the beautiful complexity of your artful creation— gladly follow the meaningful course of your gigantic, luminous clock—fathom the due proportion of forces and the laws of the wondrous workings of countless realms and their seasons. But true to Night shall remain my secret heart, and to Creative Love, her daughter. Can *you* show me a heart forever true? Has your sun eyes that look upon me in friendly recognition? Do your stars grasp the hand I extend in longing? Do they return its gentle pressure or a tender word? Was it you who embellished Her with colors and bright outline—or was it She who gave your adornment higher, more precious significance? What delight, what pleasure can your life offer that would equal Death's raptures? Does not all that inspires us wear the color of Night? She holds you like a mother and to her you owe all your splendor. You would vanish in yourself— perish in endless space—if she did not hold you, bind you, so that you grow warm and in flame beget the world. Truly, I was before you were—the Mother sent me with my brothers and sisters to inhabit your world, to sanctify it with love, that it might become a monument made eternal by our viewing—to plant it with flowers that never wilt. As yet they have not come to fruition, these divine thoughts—as yet the traces of our revelation are few—But one day your clock will mark the end of time, then you will become as one of us, and full of longing and fervor, quench your fire and die. In myself I feel the end of your busy-ness—heavenly freedom, blessed return. In my wild pain I perceive how distant you still are from our home, recognize your resistance to the ancient rule of heaven. Your wrath and your raging are vain. Unconsumable stands the Cross—a victory banner of our race.

> I pilgrim onward
> And every pain

Wird einst ein Stachel
Der Wollust sein.

Noch wenig Zeiten,
So bin ich los
Und liege trunken
Der Lieb im Schoß.

Unendliches Leben
Wogt mächtig in mir,
Ich schaue von oben
Herunter nach dir.

An jenem Hügel
Verlischt dein Glanz—
Ein Schatten bringet
Den kühlenden Kranz.

O! sauge, Geliebter,
Gewaltig mich an,
Das ich entschlummern
Und lieben kann.

Ich fühle des Todes
Verjüngende Flut,
Zu Balsam und Äther
Verwandelt mein Blut—

Ich lebe bei Tage
Voll Glauben und Mut
Und sterbe die Nächte
In heiliger Glut.

V

Über der Menschen weitverbreitete Stämme herrschte vorzeiten ein
eisernes Schicksal mit stummer Gewalt. Eine dunkle, schwere Binde
lag um ihre bange Seele—unendlich war die Erde—der Götter
Aufenthalt und ihre Heimat. Seit Ewigkeiten stand ihr geheimnisvoller Bau. Über des Morgens roten Bergen, in des Meeres heili-

Shall once be surety
Of greater gain.

Short is the time
Until I am free,
Drunken with joy
In Love's lap to be.

Life unending
Within me flows,
From above I gaze
On thee here below.

On the mound of that grave
Thy splendor shall cease,
And a shadow extend
The green cooling wreath.

O, tug at me mightily,
Dearly beloved,
That I may slumber
Forever to love.

Within me I feel
Death's youth-giving flood
To balsam and ether
Transforming my blood.

By day do I live
Full of faith and desire,
At night then to die
In heavenly fire.

V

Over the far-flung races of men there reigned in ages past an iron
fate with silent might. A dark, oppressive bond lay upon the anxious soul of man—Infinite was the earth—the sojourn of the gods,
and their home. From eternity had its mysterious fabric stood.
Above morning's red mountains, in the sea's holy womb dwelt the

gem Schoß wohnte die Sonne, das allzündende, lebendige Licht. Ein
alter Riese trug die selige Welt. Fest unter Bergen lagen die Ur-
söhne der Mutter Erde. Ohnmächtig in ihrer zerstörenden Wut gegen das neue herrliche Göttergeschlecht und dessen Verwandten,
die fröhlichen Menschen. Des Meers dunkle, grüne Tiefe war einer
Göttin Schoß. In den kristallenen Grotten schwelgte ein üppiges
Volk. Flüsse, Bäume, Blumen und Tiere hatten menschlichen Sinn.
Süßer schmeckte der Wein, von sichtbarer Jugendfülle geschenkt—
ein Gott in den Trauben—eine liebende, mütterliche Göttin, em-
porwachsend in vollen goldenen Garben—der Liebe heilger Rausch
ein süßer Dienst der schönsten Götterfrau—ein ewig buntes Fest
der Himmelskinder und der Erdbewohner, rauschte das Leben, wie
ein Frühling, durch die Jahrhunderte hin—. Alle Geschlechter ver-
ehrten kindlich die zarte, tausendfältige Flamme als das Höchste
der Welt. *Ein* Gedanke nur war es, *ein* entsetzliches Traumbild,

> Das furchtbar zu den frohen Tischen trat
> Und das Gemüt in wilde Schrecken hüllte.
> Hier wußten selbst die Götter keinen Rat,
> Der die beklommne Brust mit Trost erfüllte.
> Geheimnisvoll war dieses Unholds Pfad,
> Des Wut kein Flehn und keine Gabe stillte;
> Es war der Tod, der dieses Lustgelag
> Mit Angst und Schmerz und Tränen unterbrach.

> Auf ewig nun von allem abgeschieden,
> Was hier das Herz in süßer Wollust regt,
> Getrennt von den Geliebten, die hienieden
> Vergebne Sehnsucht, langes Weh bewegt,
> Schien matter Traum dem Toten nur beschieden,
> Ohnmächtges Ringen nur ihm auferlegt.
> Zerbrochen war die Woge des Genusses
> Am Felsen des unendlichen Verdrusses.

> Mit kühnem Geist und hoher Sinnenglut
> Verschönte sich der Mensch die grause Larve,
> Ein sanfter Jüngling löscht das Licht und ruht—
> Sanft wird das Ende, wie ein Wehn der Harfe.
> Erinnrung schmilzt in kühler Schattenflut,

sun, the all-kindling, living Light. An ancient giant bore up the blissful world. Imprisoned beneath mountains lay the primal sons of Mother Earth—impotent in their destructive rage against the new lordly race of gods and their kin, happy mankind. The sea's dark green depths were the womb of a goddess. In crystalline grottoes reveled a thriving race. Rivers, trees, flowers, and animals had human meaning. Sweeter tasted the wine poured by Youth's visible fullness—a god in the grape—a loving, maternal goddess, growing up in the full golden grain—Love's holy intoxication a sweet attendance upon the most beautiful of divine women—an eternally gay festival of the children of heaven and the inhabitants of earth, life moved like a rushing stream, like springtime, through the centuries—With childlike awe all races venerated the tender, thousandfold flame as the highest thing in the world. Only *one* thought, *one* terrifying vision

All-baleful to this happy banquet came
And sank the heart in uncontrollèd fear.
Here knew the gods themselves no spell to tame,
Nor any comfort for the anxious ear.
Unerring was this monster's fearsome aim,
Whose course no prayer or sacrifice could veer;
Aye, Death it was broke up this merry rout
With anguish, pain, and sobbing all about.

Forever parted now from every show
That stirs the heart to sweet voluptuousness,
Cut off from those beloved, whom here below
Vain longing moves and weary woefulness,
Pale dreams were all the dead man now could know,
Though struggling still in piteous powerlessness.
Dashed was the wave on sensual pleasure bent
Against the rock of endless discontent.

With daring mind, at ardent senses hest,
Men sought the gruesome countenance to conceal:
A gentle youth turns down his torch and rests;
The end is tender—a harp's last faint appeal.
In shadowy stream from them is memory wrest—

So sang das Lied dem traurigen Bedarfe.
Doch unenträtselt blieb die ewge Nacht,
Das ernste Zeichen einer fernen Macht.

Zu Ende neigte die alte Welt sich. Des jungen Geschlechts Lust-
garten verwelkte—hinauf in den freieren, wüsten Raum strebten
die unkindlichen, wachsenden Menschen. Die Götter verschwan-
den mit ihrem Gefolge—einsam und leblos stand die Natur. Mit
eiserner Kette band sie die dürre Zahl und das strenge Maß. Wie
in Staub und Lüfte zerfiel in dunkle Worte die unermeßliche Blüte
des Lebens. Entflohn war der beschwörende Glauben und die all-
verwandelnde, allverschwisternde Himmelsgenossin, die Phanta-
sie. Unfreundlich blies ein kalter Nordwind über die erstarrte Flur,
und die erstarrte Wunderheimat verflog in den Äther. Des Himmels Fernen füllten mit leuchtenden Welten sich. Ins tiefre Heilig-
tum, in des Gemüts höhern Raum zog mit ihren Mächten die Seele
der Welt—zu walten dort bis zum Anbruch der tagenden
Weltherrlichkeit. Nicht mehr war das Licht der Götter Aufenthalt
und himmlisches Zeichen—den Schleier der Nacht warfen sie über
sich. Die Nacht ward der Offenbarungen mächtiger Schoß—in ihn
kehrten die Götter zurück—schlummerten ein, um in neuen, herr-
lichern Gestalten auszugehn über die veränderte Welt. Im Volk, das,
vor allen verachtet, zu früh reif und der seligen Unschuld der Jugend trotzig fremd geworden war, erschien mit nie gesehenem Angesicht die neue Welt—In der Armut dichterischer Hütte—Ein Sohn
der ersten Jungfrau und Mutter—Geheimnisvoller Umarmung
unendliche Frucht. Des Morgenlands ahndende, blütenreiche
Weisheit erkannte zuerst der neuen Zeit Beginn—Zu des Königs
demütiger Wiege wies ihr ein Stern den Weg. In der weiten Zukunft Namen huldigten sie ihm mit Glanz und Duft, den höchsten
Wundern der Natur. Einsam entfaltete das himmlische Herz sich
zu einem Blütenkelch allmächtiger Liebe—des Vaters hohem Antlitz zugewandt und ruhend an dem ahndungsselgen Busen der
lieblich ernsten Mutter. Mit vergötternder Inbrunst schaute das
weissagende Auge des blühenden Kindes auf die Tage der Zukunft, nach seinen Geliebten, den Sprossen seines Götterstamms,
unbekümmert über seiner Tage irdisches Schicksal. Bald sammel-
ten die kindlichsten Gemüter, von inniger Liebe wundersam er-
griffen, sich um ihn her. Wie Blumen keimte ein neues, fremdes

So ran the chant man's sorry need to heal.
But still unriddled was eternal Night,
The earnest symbol of a distant might.

The old world was declining toward its end. The pleasure garden of the young race was withering—upwards, into freer, barren
space strove the unchildlike, maturing race of men. The gods vanished with their train—lonely and lifeless stood Nature. Arid number and strict measure bound her with iron chains. As into dust
and thin air the immeasurable bloom of life crumbled and evapo-
rated into dark words. Fled was invoking belief and its heavenly
companion, creative imagination, which transforms all and makes
all kin. A cold north wind blew inimically over the benumbed
landscape, and the benumbed home of marvels vanished into the
ether. Cosmic spaces began to be filled with luminous worlds. Into
a deeper sanctuary, into the higher realm of mind and heart, withdrew the soul of the world and its powers—to hold sway there
until the dawn of its universal dominion. No longer was Light the
sojourning place of the gods and a heaven-sent sign—these had
thrown the veil of Night about them. Night became the mighty
womb of revelations—into it the gods returned—fell asleep, to rise
again in new, more splendid form and go forth into the changed
world. In the midst of a people who—despised above all others—
had matured too early and grown defiantly alienated from the
blessed innocence of youth—there appeared with never before seen
countenance the new world—In poverty's poetic cot—A son of the
first virgin and mother—Infinite fruit of mysterious embrace. The
Orient's foreknowing, fertile wisdom was the first to recognize the
beginning of the new age—To the King's humble cradle a star
showed it the way. In the name of the distant future it paid homage to him with brilliance and fragrance, Nature's highest marvels.
In solitude the heavenly heart unfolded to a blossom cup of almighty Love—turned toward his Father's regal face and resting on
the presciently blissful bosom of his sweetly earnest Mother. With
adoring fervor the prophetic eye of the flourishing child gazed upon
the days of the future, toward his loved ones, the branches of his
vine, untroubled by the earthly fate awaiting him. Soon the most
childlike hearts, strangely moved by ardent Love, gathered about
him. A strange new life budded like flowers in his presence. Words

Leben in seiner Nähe. Unerschöpfliche Worte und der Botschaften fröhlichste fielen wie Funken eines göttlichen Geistes von seinen freundlichen Lippen. Von ferner Küste, unter Hellas' heiterm Himmel geboren, kam ein Sänger nach Palästina und ergab sein ganzes Herz dem Wunderkinde:

> Der Jüngling bist du, der seit langer Zeit
> Auf unsern Gräbern steht in tiefem Sinnen;
> Ein tröstlich Zeichen in der Dunkelheit—
> Der höhern Menschheit freudiges Beginnen.
> Was uns gesenkt in tiefe Traurigkeit,
> Zieht uns mit süßer Sehnsucht nun von hinnen.
> Im Tode ward das ewge Leben kund,
> Du bist der Tod und machst uns erst gesund.

Der Sänger zog voll Freudigkeit nach Indostan—das Herz von süßer Liebe trunken; und schüttete in feurigen Gesängen es unter jenem milden Himmel aus, daß tausend Herzen sich zu ihm neigten und die fröhliche Botschaft tausendzweigig emporwuchs. Bald nach des Sängers Abschied ward das köstliche Leben ein Opfer des menschlichen tiefen Verfalls—Er starb in jungen Jahren, weggerissen von der geliebten Welt, von der weinenden Mutter und seinen zagenden Freunden. Der unsäglichen Leiden dunkeln Kelch leerte der liebliche Mund—In entsetzlicher Angst nahte die Stunde der Geburt der neuen Welt. Hart rang er mit des alten Todes Schrecken—Schwer lag der Druck der alten Welt auf ihm. Noch einmal sah er freundlich nach der Mutter—da kam der ewigen Liebe lösende Hand—und er entschlief. Nur wenig Tage hing ein tiefer Schleier über das brausende Meer, über das bebende Land—unzählige Tränen weinten die Geliebten—Entsiegelt ward das Geheimnis—himmlische Geister hoben den uralten Stein vom dunkeln Grabe. Engel saßen bei dem Schlummernden—aus seinen Träumen zart gebildet—Erwacht in neuer Götterherrlichkeit, erstieg er die Höhe der neugebornen Welt—begrub mit eigner Hand den alten Leichnam in die verlaßne Höhle und legte mit allmächtiger Hand den Stein, den keine Macht erhebt, darauf.

Noch weinen deine Lieben Tränen der Freude, Tränen der Rührung und des unendlichen Danks an deinem Grabe—sehn dich noch immer, freudig erschreckt, auferstehn—und sich mit dir; sehn

of inexhaustible wisdom and the happiest of all messages fell like sparks of a divine spirit from his kindly lips. From a distant shore, born under the serene sky of Hellas, a singer came to Palestine and gave his whole heart to the miraculous child:

> Thou art the youth who for long ages stood
> Upon our graves with pensive face—
> A ray of comfort in our darkest mood
> And joyful harbinger of a higher race.
> What once all happiness could but exclude
> Now draws us with sweet longing on apace.
> In death dost thou of life eternal tell,
> For thou art death now come to make us well.

The singer journeyed joyfully to Hindustan—and poured out his heart drunken with sweet Love in fiery hymns under that mild sky, so that thousands of hearts bowed to him, and the glad tidings sprang up thousand-branched. Soon after the singer's departure precious life became the victim of human depravity.—He died still young, torn from the world he loved, from his weeping mother and his faint-hearted friends. The dear mouth emptied the dark cup of unutterable suffering—In terrible anxiety the hour for the new world to be born drew near. He struggled hard with the terrors of the old Death—Heavy lay the weight of the old world upon him. Once more he looked with kindly eyes at his mother—then came eternal Love's releasing hand—and he fell asleep. Only for a few days did a deep veil hang over the raging sea and the trembling land—his loved ones wept countless tears—Unsealed was the mystery—heavenly spirits raised the age-old stone from the dark grave. Angels were sitting by the slumberer—tenderly formed from his dreams—Awakened in new divine magnificence he ascended the height of the newborn world—buried with his own hand the corpse of the old world in the deserted cavern and laid upon it with almighty hand the stone no power can raise.

Still do your loved ones weep tears of joy, tears of compassion and unending gratitude at your grave—joyously startled, they still see you rise—and themselves with you; see you weep with sweet fervor on your mother's blessed bosom, earnestly walk with friends,

dich weinen mit süßer Inbrunst an der Mutter seligem Busen, ernst mit den Freunden wandeln, Worte sagen, wie vom Baum des Lebens gebrochen; sehen dich eilen mit voller Sehnsucht in des Vaters Arm, bringend die junge Menschheit, und der goldnen Zukunft unversieglichen Becher. Die Mutter eilte bald dir nach—in himmlischem Triumph—Sie war die erste in der neuen Heimat bei dir. Lange Zeiten entflossen seitdem, und in immer höherm Glanze regte deine neue Schöpfung sich—und Tausende zogen aus Schmerzen und Qualen, voll Glauben und Sehnsucht und Treue dir nach—walten mit dir und der himmlischen Jungfrau im Reiche der Liebe—dienen im Tempel des himmlischen Todes und sind in Ewigkeit dein.

Gehoben ist der Stein—
Die Menschheit ist erstanden—
Wir alle bleiben dein
Und fühlen keine Banden.
Der herbste Kummer fleucht
Vor deiner goldnen Schale,
Wenn Erd und Leben weicht
Im letzten Abendmahle.

Zur Hochzeit ruft der Tod—
Die Lampen brennen helle—
Die Jungfraun sind zur Stelle—
Um Öl ist keine Not—
Erklänge doch die Ferne
Von deinem Zuge schon,
Und ruften uns die Sterne
Mit Menschenzung' und Ton.

Nach dir, Maria, heben
Schon tausend Herzen sich.
In diesem Schattenleben
Verlangten sie nur dich.
Sie hoffen zu genesen
Mit ahndungsvoller Lust—
Drückst du sie, heilges Wesen,
An deine treue Brust.

uttering words as though broken from the tree of life; see you has-
ten full of longing into the arms of the Father, bringing with you
young mankind, and the cup of the golden future that never runs
dry. Your mother soon hastened to join you—in heavenly triumph—
She was the first in the new home with you. Long ages have passed
since then, and in ever higher glory did your new creation stir—
thousands followed after you out of pain and torment, full of faith
and longing and loyalty—to reign with you and the heavenly Virgin in the kingdom of Love—to serve in the temple of heavenly
Death and be yours in eternity.

Uplifted is the stone—
And mankind is arisen—
We all shall be thine own
And feel no mortal prison.
The bitterest sorrow flees
Before thy golden cup,
When earth and life recede
And we take final sup.

To wed him Death invites us—
The lamps are burning brightly—
The virgins present nightly—
No lack of oil to light us—
Oh, if but in the distance
Resounded now thy train,
If but the stars' insistence
Had human tongue and strain!

To thee, O Virgin Mother,
A thousand hearts are raised.
In this shadow-life no other
But only thee they praised.
They hope now to recover—
With prescient joy they're blest—
If, thou, O Holy Mother,
Dost press them to thy breast.

So manche, die sich glühend
In bittrer Qual verzehrt
Und dieser Welt entfliehend
Nach dir sich hingekehrt;
Die hülfreich uns erschienen
In mancher Not und Pein—
Wir kommen nun zu ihnen,
Um ewig da zu sein.

Nun weint an keinem Grabe
Für Schmerz, wer liebend glaubt.
Der Liebe süße Habe
Wird keinem nicht geraubt—
Die Sehnsucht ihm zu lindern,
Begeistert ihn die Nacht—
Von treuen Himmelskindern
Wird ihm sein Herz bewacht.

Getrost, das Leben schreitet
Zum ewgen Leben hin;
Von innrer Glut geweitet,
Verklärt sich unser Sinn.
Die Sternwelt wird zerfließen
Zum goldnen Lebenswein,
Wir werden sie genießen
Und lichte Sterne sein.

Die Lieb ist frei gegeben
Und keine Trennung mehr.
Es wogt das volle Leben
Wie ein unendlich Meer.
Nur *eine* Nacht der Wonne—
Ein ewiges Gedicht—
Und unser aller Sonne
Ist Gottes Angesicht.

So many, in pain burning,
Consumed with bitter grief,
From this world sadly turning,
In thee found sweet relief.
Those who, our pain to lighten,
With us did firm abide—
We come their joy to heighten,
Eternal at their side.

At no grave weeps heartbroken
Who lives in sure belief,
And blessèd Love's sweet token
Is safe from every thief.
Inspired by Night, our longing
Is constantly allayed—
Our hearts from earthly wronging
By heaven's children stayed.

Take comfort, life progresses
On to eternal life;
An inward fire's excesses
Make inward senses ripe.
The star-world deliquescing
Will yield life's golden wine
And we, that world possessing,
As dartling stars shall shine.

Love has been given freedom,
No parting more can be.
Life's surging in our bosom
Is like a boundless sea.
One night of bliss eternal—
One poem without end—
And there our sun supernal
Does God's own visage lend.

VI

Sehnsucht nach dem Tode

Hinunter in der Erde Schoß,
Weg aus des Lichtes Reichen,
Der Schmerzen Wut und wilder Stoß
Ist froher Abfahrt Zeichen.
Wir kommen in dem engen Kahn
Geschwind am Himmelsufer an.

Gelobt sei uns die ewge Nacht,
Gelobt der ewge Schlummer.
Wohl hat der Tag uns warm gemacht
Und welk der lange Kummer.
Die Lust der Fremde ging uns aus,
Zum Vater wollen wir nach Haus.

Was sollen wir auf dieser Welt
Mit unsrer Lieb und Treue?
Das Alte wird hintangestellt,
Was soll uns dann das Neue?
O! einsam steht und tiefbetrübt,
Wer heiß und fromm die Vorzeit liebt.

Die Vorzeit, wo die Sinne licht
In hohen Flammen brannten,
Des Vaters Hand und Angesicht
Die Menschen noch erkannten.
Und hohen Sinns, einfältiglich
Noch mancher seinem Urbild glich.

Die Vorzeit, wo noch blütenreich
Uralte Stämme prangten
Und Kinder für das Himmelreich
Nach Qual und Tod verlangten.
Und wenn auch Lust und Leben sprach,
Doch manches Herz für Liebe brach.

VI

Longing for Death

Now down into the womb of earth,
Away from this Light's kingdom,
Our raging pain and sense of dearth
But hail a new dominion;
And sailing in our narrow bark
We'll soon the shores of heaven mark.

Let us now praise eternal Night,
And praise eternal slumber.
The heat of day has sapped our might,
Long sorrows without number.
To dwell abroad has lost its charms,
We long for home, our Father's arms.

What good to us a world like this?
What hope of true Love's sharing?
What was of yore is now dismissed,
The new leaves us uncaring.
Oh, sad and lonely evermore
Whose heart is with the days of yore!

The days of yore, when senses bright
In highest flame were burning,
And mankind still was sound of sight,
God's face and hand discerning;
Then lofty mind and simple heart
Still many with God's image marked.

The days of yore, when ancient clans
In fullest bloom still flourished,
And children, to gain heaven's strand,
The hope of torment nourished.
Though worldly joy and life still spake,
Full many a heart for Love did break.

Die Vorzeit, wo in Jugendglut
Gott selbst sich kundgegeben
Und frühem Tod in Liebesmut
Geweiht sein süßes Leben.
Und Angst und Schmerz nicht von sich trieb,
Damit er uns nur teuer blieb.

Mit banger Sehnsucht sehn wir sie
In dunkle Nacht gehüllet;
In dieser Zeitlichkeit wird nie
Der heiße Durst gestillet.
Wir müssen nach der Heimat gehn,
Um diese heilge Zeit zu sehn.

Was hält noch unsre Rückkehr auf,
Die Liebsten ruhn schon lange.
Ihr Grab schließt unsern Lebenslauf,
Nun wird uns weh und bange.
Zu suchen haben wir nichts mehr—
Das Herz ist satt—die Welt ist leer.

Unendlich und geheimnisvoll
Durchströmt uns süßer Schauer—
Mir deucht, aus tiefen Fernen scholl
Ein Echo unsrer Trauer.
Die Lieben sehnen sich wohl auch
Und sandten uns der Sehnsucht Hauch.

Hinunter zu der süßen Braut,
Zu Jesus, dem Geliebten—
Getrost, die Abenddämmrung graut
Den Liebenden, Betrübten.
Ein Traum bricht unsre Banden los
Und senkt uns in des Vaters Schoß.

The days of yore, when God himself
In prime of youth descended,
And out of Love his blessèd self
To early death commended;
And from him drove not fear and pain
That ours might be the dearer gain.

With yearning sick those times we see
In darkest Night concealèd.
This realm of time we sure must flee
Ere our pain can be healèd.
We must our way straight homeward wend
To see those holy times again.

What still impedes our swift return?
Our loved ones long are resting.
Their grave is our own mortal bourn,
Our fears grow more distressing.
We've nothing more to look for here—
The heart is full—the world is sere.

In infinite and secret wise
A thrill of awe steals through us—
I think I heard from distant skies
An echo of our sadness.
Our loved ones must feel longing too—
Their longing keeps our longing true.

So down then to the blessèd bride,
To Jesus, the belovèd,
Take comfort, evening shades abide
About his grieving lovers.
A dream will break our bonds apart
And sink us in the Father's heart.

R. M. Browning

Ludwig Tieck

Liebe

Liebe denkt in süßen Tönen,
Denn Gedanken stehn zu fern,
Nur in Tönen mag sie gern
Alles, was sie will, verschönen.
Drum ist ewig uns zugegen,
Wenn Musik mit Klängen spricht,
Ihr die Sprache nicht gebricht,
Holde Lieb auf allen Wegen;
Liebe kann sich nicht bewegen,
Leihet sie den Odem nicht.

Clemens Brentano

Der Spinnerin Lied

Es sang vor langen Jahren
Wohl auch die Nachtigall,
Das war wohl süßer Schall,
Da wir zusammen waren.

Ich sing und kann nicht weinen
Und spinne so allein
Den Faden klar und rein,
Solang der Mond wird scheinen.

Da wir zusammen waren,
Da sang die Nachtigall,

Ludwig Tieck

Love

Love must think in music sweetly,
for all thought is too remote.
Only music can denote
all that love desires completely.
Love we know and know her only
when the voice of music sounds;
while her magic still abounds,
love can never leave us lonely.
Love would die a sterile death,
did not music lend her breath.

Herman Salinger

Clemens Brentano

The Spinstress' Song

Of yore, as now, aringing
Sweet sang the nightingale.
We heard the echo trail,
Each to the other clinging.

I sing to keep from weeping
And spin, all lonesome here,
The thread so pure and clear
Until the moon sets, sleeping.

Each to the other clinging
We heard the nightingale.

Nun mahnet mich ihr Schall,
Daß du von mir gefahren.

So oft der Mond mag scheinen,
Gedenk ich dein allein,
Mein Herz ist klar und rein,
Gott wolle uns vereinen!

Seit du von mir gefahren,
Singt stets die Nachtigall,
Ich denk bei ihrem Schall,
Wie wir zusammen waren.

Gott wolle uns vereinen,
Hier spinn ich so allein,
Der Mond scheint klar und rein,
Ich sing und möchte weinen!

Abendständchen

Hör, es klagt die Flöte wieder,
Und die kühlen Brunnen rauschen.
Golden wehn die Töne nieder,
Stille, stille, laß uns lauschen!

Holdes Bitten, mild Verlangen,
Wie es süß zum Herzen spricht!
Durch die Nacht, die mich umfangen,
Blickt zu mir der Töne Licht.

Wenn ich ein Bettelmann wär'
Käm' ich zu Dir,
Säh' Dich gar bittend an
Was gäbst Du mir?—

But now the echoes trail,
For you did leave me, singing.

Ere yet the moon sets sleeping,
My thoughts roam far from here.
My heart is pure and clear.
God joins us in His keeping.

Since you did leave me, singing,
I hear the nightingale.
We heard the echoes trail,
Faintly together clinging.

God joins us in His keeping.
I spin, all lonesome here,
The moon shines pure and clear,
I sing and would be weeping.

Alexander Gode

Serenade

Harken how the flute complains,
And the fountains plash and glisten!
Music drifts in golden rains;
Softly, softly let us listen!

Gentle-pleading, mild desire
Sweetly tells the heart its plight!
Through the darkness, bright as fire,
Gleams upon me—music's light.

Herman Salinger

If I were a beggarman,
To you I'd flee;
My eyes would plead with you:
Something for me?

Der Pfennig hilft mir nicht
Nimm ihn zurück,
Goldner als golden glänzt
Allen Dein Blick;

Und was Du allen gibst
Gebe nicht mir
Nur was mein Aug' begehrt
Will ich von Dir.

Bettler wie half' ich Dir?—
Sprächst Du nur so,
Dann wär' im Herzen ich
Glücklich und froh.

Laufst auf Dein Kämmerlein
Holst ein Paar Schuh
Die sind mir viel zu klein,
Sieh einmal zu.—

Sieh nur wie klein sie sind
Drücken mich sehr,
Jungfrau süß lächelst Du,
O gib mir mehr.

Am Berge hoch in Lüften,
Da baute er sein Haus;
Am Tore liegt Gewitter,
Nun kann er nicht hinaus.
Die Wolken, sie wollen nicht ziehen,
Der Pfad ist steil und schwer,
O Lieber, Herzlieber in Lüften,
O wenn ich bei Dir wär'!

Your penny cannot help,
No, not a chance.
Golder than golden gleams
On all men your glance.

But what you give to all,
Don't give me too.
Only what my eye desires
I seek from you.

Beggar, how may I help?—
Should you speak so,
Then in my heart I'd feel
Happiness glow.

Off to your bedroom
To fetch some old shoes?
They're much too small for me,
Simply won't do.

Just look how tight they are,
Make my feet sore;
Maiden, your smile is kind,
O, give me more!

David B. Dickens

Adieu, Heart's Love, Adieu!

He built upon the mountain
　　That rises in the North;
The tempest roars around him,
　　And will not let him forth.
The clouds are full of blackness,
　　The path is steep and bare,
O heart's love on the mountain,
　　O would with thee I were!

Wohl bei Dir über Wolken,
Wohl bei Dir über Wind,
Wo fromme Vöglein schweben
In Himmelsluft so lind.
Meine Flüglein, die sind mir gebrochen
Und heilen auch nicht eh'
Bis ich zu der Herzliebsten
Durch Tür und Tor eingeh'!

Daß ich so stolz in Lüften
Mein Haus gebauet hab',
Das muß mich gar betrüben,
Ich kann nicht mehr hinab;
Die Riegel sind alle verrostet,
Die Tore sie gehen so schwer,
O Liebchen, Herzliebchen im Tale,
O wenn ich bei Dir wär'!

Wohl bei Dir in dem Garten,
Wohl bei Dir in dem Wald,
Wo dichte Bäume stehen
Und Vogelsang erschallt.
Ich kann kein' Kranz mehr flechten
Und singen auch nicht eh'
Bis ich zu Dir Herzliebste
Durch Flur and Wald eingeh'.

Sie dringt wohl durch die Wolken,
Geht ein durch Tür und Tor,
Die Flüglein schnell ihr heilen
Und heben sie empor,
Wohl über die Wolken und höher
Zu Gott wohl in die Höh',
Trägt sie das treue Herze,
Ade, Herzlieber, ade!—

Er dringt wohl durch die Wolke,
Geht ein durch Flur und Wald,
Ein Kranz wird ihm geflochten,

O fair upon the mountain,
  Above the cloud and blast,
Where sky is warm and sunlit,
  And eagles hurry past!
My wings, alas! are broken,
  And lift me not, before
I go unto my heart's love,
  And enter at his door.

That I have built my dwelling
  High on the mountain's crown,
Alas! 'tis all my sorrow,
  No more may I come down.
The bolts and bars are rusted,
  And crumbled is the stair.
O heart's love in the valley,
  O would with thee I were!

O fair within the garden!
  O fair within the grove!
Where birds upon the branches
  Are signing of their love!
No flower have I to garland,
  No song to sing, before
I go unto my heart's love,
  And enter at her door.

And up the steep she presses,
  Nor heeds the bolts and bars,
And now her soul is wingèd,
  And borne up to the stars;
And higher yet, and higher
  To Him up in the blue,
Her faithful heart she carries,—
  Adieu, heart's love, adieu!

And down the steep he presses,
  And through the wood he goes,
And hears the shepherds' music,

Ein Lied ihm auch erschallt,
Wohl unter dem Baum und wohl tiefer
Wohl unter grünem Klee
Ruht nun sein stolzes Herze,
Ade, Herzliebste, ade!—

Heil'ge Nacht, heil'ge Nacht!
Sterngeschloßner Himmelsfrieden!
Alles, was das Licht geschieden,
Ist verbunden,
Alle Wunden
Bluten süß im Abendrot!

Bjelbogs Speer, Bjelbogs Speer
Sinkt ins Herz der trunknen Erde,
Die mit seliger Geberde
Eine Rose
In dem Schoße
Dunkler Lüste niedertaucht.

Zücht'ge Braut, zücht'ge Braut!
Deine süße Schmach verhülle,
Wenn des Hochzeitbechers Fülle
Sich ergießet.
Also fließet
In die brünst'ge Nacht der Tag!

Nachklänge Beethovenscher Musik

I

Einsamkeit, du stummer Bronnen,
Heil'ge Mutter tiefer Quellen,
Zauberspiegel innrer Sonnen,

And sees the blowing rose.
And deeper yet, and deeper
  Beneath the grass and dew
His haughty heart reposes,—
  Adieu, heart's love, adieu!

Richard Garnett

Holy night, holy night!
Star-made peace of heav'nly wonder,
All that light has torn asunder
One and bound now
And all wounds now
Sweetly bleed in evening's red.

Bjelbog's speer, Bjelbog's speer,
Drunken earth's heart penetrating,
Earth with blissful celebrating,
Rose aglow,
In lust's tow,
Sinks within the womb of dark.

Modest bride, modest bride!
Your sweet shame must now surrender
When the wedding cup is tendered
Brimming over!
Thus brims over
Into ardent night the day.

David B. Dickens

Echoes of Beethoven's Music

I
Sacred mother of deep springs,
Solitude, oh silent well,
Mirror of the inner suns

Die in Tönen überschwellen,
Seit ich durft' in deine Wonnen
Das betörte Leben stellen,
Seit du ganz mich überronnen
Mit den dunklen Wunderwellen,
Hab' zu funkeln ich begonnen,
Und nun klingen all die hellen
Sternensphären meiner Seele,
Deren Takt ein Gott mir zähle.
Alle Sonnen meines Herzens,
Die Planeten meiner Lust,
Die Kometen meines Schmerzens
Klingen hoch in meiner Brust.
In dem Monde meiner Wehmut,
Alles Glanzes unbewußt,
Muß ich singen und in Demut
Vor den Schätzen meines Innern,
Vor der Armut meines Lebens,
Vor den Gipfeln meines Strebens,
Ewiger Gott! mich dein erinnern.
Alles andre ist vergebens!

II

Gott! dein Himmel faßt mich in den Haaren,
Deine Erde reißt mich in die Hölle.
Herr, wo soll ich doch mein Herz bewahren,
Daß ich deine Schwelle sicher stelle—
Also fleh' ich durch die Nacht. Da fließen
Meine Klagen hin wie Feuerbronnen,
Die mit glühenden Meeren mich umschließen.
Doch inmitten hab' ich Grund gewonnen,
Rage hoch gleich rätselvollen Riesen,
Memnons Bild. Des Morgens erste Sonnen
Fragend ihren Strahl zur Stirn mir schießen,
Und den Traum, den Mitternacht gesponnen,
Üb' ich tönend, um den Tag zu grüßen.

III

Selig, wer ohne Sinne
Schwebt wie ein Geist auf dem Wasser,

Which, imaged, into music swell.
Since the time when I put down
My errors on your blissful path,
Since the time I wholly drowned
Within your dark and wondrous bath,
I am endued in glitter's gown.
For what rings bright in me, the staff
Of a god may count the beat and bars,
A soul's song of circling stars.
The suns that in my heart have shone,
The planets that my rapture share,
The comets that my anguish own,
Play in my breast their full-toned air.
In my melancholy's moon,
Of every splendor unaware,
Humble I must sing out my tune
At treasures hidden deep within me,
At hardships where my life is caught,
At peaks for which my quest has sought,
And, eternal God, recall Thee!
All else would be done for naught.

II

Oh God, hair-seized, your heaven lifts me high,
And yet your earth to hell must drag me down,
Oh Lord, in what cache shall my heart abide,
That I may sure and safe your threshold own?
Thus I pray hot throughout the night, my cries
Flow ceaseless like a fire-well's burning band,
And make me captive, caught in flaming seas,
And yet, among them, I've a place to stand,
Like unto cryptic giant forms I rise,
A Memnon's statue: morning's first suns send
Their querying beams as arrows at my mind,
And dreams which from the midnight's loom descend
I weave to greet the day in music's kind.

III

Blessed the man who, senses shorn,
Hovers like a spirit over the waters.

Nicht wie ein Schiff—die Flaggen
Wechselnd der Zeit, und Segel
Blähend, wie heute der Wind weht.
Nein, ohne Sinne, dem Gott gleich,
Selbst sich nur wissend und dichtend
Schafft er die Welt, die er selbst ist,
Und es sündigt der Mensch drauf,
Und es war nicht sein Wille!
Aber geteilet ist alles.
Keinem ward alles, denn jedes
Hat einen Herrn, nur der Herr nicht.
Einsam ist er und dient nicht.
So auch der Sänger.

Joseph Freiherr von Eichendorff

Wünschelrute

Schläft ein Lied in allen Dingen,
Die da träumen fort und fort,
Und die Welt hebt an zu singen,
Triffst du nur das Zauberwort.

Das zerbrochene Ringlein

In einem kühlen Grunde
Da geht ein Mühlenrad,
Mein' Liebste ist verschwunden,
Die dort gewohnet hat.

And shifts not flags with time
As a ship does, unfurling
Sails to catch the winds the day may bring.
No, senses shorn likest unto God,
Knowing but himself, creating,
He makes the world that he himself is,
And mankind sins upon it,
And it was not his will!
Yet all is divided.
No one is vouchsafed all, for each thing
Has a lord set to it, save the Lord;
Alone He stands, and serves not.
Thus, too, the singer.

G. C. Schoolfield

Joseph Freiherr von Eichendorff

Divining Rod

Slumb'ring deep in every thing
Dreams a song as yet unheard,
And the world begins to sing
If you find the magic word.

Alison Turner

The Broken Ring

Within a watered valley
  A mill turns night and day;
And there my love was dwelling
  Before she went away.

Sie hat mir Treu' versprochen,
Gab mir ein'n Ring dabei,
Sie hat die Treu' gebrochen,
Mein Ringlein sprang entzwei.

Ich möcht als Spielmann reisen
Weit in die Welt hinaus,
Und singen meine Weisen,
Und gehn von Haus zu Haus.

Ich möcht' als Reiter fliegen
Wohl in die blut'ge Schlacht,
Um stille Feuer liegen
Im Feld bei dunkler Nacht.

Hör' ich das Mühlrad gehen:
Ich weiß nicht, was ich will—
Ich möcht' am liebsten sterben,
Da wär's auf einmal still!

Der Abend

Schweigt der Menschen laute Lust:
Rauscht die Erde wie in Träumen
Wunderbar mit allen Bäumen,
Was dem Herzen kaum bewußt,
Alte Zeiten, linde Trauer,
Und es schweifen leise Schauer
Wetterleuchtend durch die Brust.

A little ring she gave me,
  A pledge to bind her heart;
But since her troth she's broken,
  My ring has come apart.

I fain would go as minstrel
  And wander far away,
And earn my bread by singing
  My songs from day to day.

I fain would mount a charger
  And glory seek in fight,
By silent camp-fires lying,
  When falls the dark of night.

For when I hear the mill-wheel,
  I know not what I will.—
I fain would die, then surely
  It would at last be still!

Geoffrey Herbert Chase

[handwritten: last 2 of Nocturne]

Evening

[Man's noisy pleasures are at rest:
From earth a dreamlike rustle rises
Through all its trees and tantalizes
The heart with strangeness half-confessed,
Times that are gone, griefs grown weaker;
Faint shiverings are felt and flicker
Like summer lightning through the breast.

[handwritten: Affect]

Edwin Morgan

Nachts

Ich wandre durch die stille Nacht,
Da schleicht der Mond so heimlich sacht
Oft aus der dunklen Wolkenhülle,
Und hin and her im Tal
Erwacht die Nachtigall,
Dann wieder alles grau und stille.

O wunderbarer Nachtgesang:
Von fern im Land der Ströme Gang,
Leis Schauern in den dunklen Bäumen—
Wirrst die Gedanken mir,
Mein irres Singen hier
Ist wie ein Rufen nur aus Träumen.

Mondnacht

Es war, als hätt' der Himmel
Die Erde still geküßt,
Daß sie im Blütenschimmer
Von ihm nun träumen müßt'.

Die Luft ging durch die Felder
Die Ähren wogten sacht,
Es rauschten leis die Wälder,
So sternklar war die Nacht.

Und meine Seele spannte
Weit ihre Flügel aus,
Flog durch die stillen Lande,
Als flöge sie nach Haus.

Nocturne

I wander through the silent night;
The moon slips secret, soft, and bright
Oft from its darkening cloudy cover.
And now along the vale
    kens the nightingale
        a gray hush again spreads over.

        er-filled nocturnal song,
    en waters whisper long,
Tre   hiver as the moonlight gleams—
Under the spell you cast
My wandering song is lost
And like a calling-out of dreams. ⌐| 1st Two
        of Evening.

Herman Salinger

Night of Moon

It was, as if with kisses
    The sky the earth had stilled,
Till deep in moon-lit blossoms,
    Her dreams alone he filled.

The silent corn was swaying,
    Caressed by breezes light;
The woodlands softly rustled,
    So star-clear was the night.

And taking flight, my spirit,
    Its pinions wide outspread,
Through silent spaces soaring,
    As though it homeward sped.

Geoffrey Herbert Chase

Sehnsucht

Es schienen so golden die Sterne,
Am Fenster ich einsam stand
Und hörte aus weiter Ferne
Ein Posthorn im stillen Land.
Das Herz mir im Leib entbrennte,
Da hab' ich mir heimlich gedacht:
Ach, wer da mitreisen könnte
In der prächtigen Sommernacht!

Zwei junge Gesellen gingen
Vorüber am Bergeshang,
Ich hörte im Wandern sie singen
Die stille Gegend entlang:
Von schwindelnden Felsenschlüften,
Wo die Wälder rauschen so sacht,
Von Quellen, die von den Klüften
Sich stürzen in die Waldesnacht.

Sie sangen von Marmorbildern,
Von Gärten, die überm Gestein
In dämmernden Lauben verwildern,
Palästen im Mondenschein,
Wo die Mädchen am Fenster lauschen,
Wann der Lauten Klang erwacht
Und die Brunnen verschlafen rauschen
In der prächtigen Sommernacht.—

Der alte Garten

Kaiserkron' und Päonien rot,
Die müssen verzaubert sein,
Denn Vater und Mutter sind lange tot,
Was blühn sie hier so allein?

Longing

So golden the stars were shining.
At the window I stood alone.
Through silent fields far echoed
A posthorn's joyous tone.
My heart caught fire, inflaming
My secret thoughts' delight:
Who would not, too, go roving
On a lovely summer's night?

And down the mountain pathway
Two youths came striding by;
The songs that they were singing
Awoke the silent sky.
They sang of rustling forests,
Where gorges meet the sight,
Of torrents downward gushing
Toward the forest's night.

They sang of marble statues,
And palaces of stone,
Of gardens in the moonlight,
Their misty bowers o'ergrown;
Where maids at casements listen,
When lutes their hearts excite,
And drowsy fountains murmur
On a lovely summer's night.

Geoffrey Herbert Chase

The Old Garden

Crown imperial and peony red,
Enchanted they appear,
My father and mother have long lain dead,
Why these lone blossoms here?

Der Springbrunn plaudert noch immerfort
Von der alten schönen Zeit,
Eine Frau sitzt eingeschlafen dort,
Ihre Locken bedecken ihr Kleid.

Sie hat eine Laute in der Hand,
Als ob sie im Schlafe spricht,
Mir ist, als hätt' ich sie sonst gekannt—
Still, geh vorbei und weck' sie nicht!

Und wenn es dunkelt das Tal entlang,
Streift sie die Saiten sacht,
Da gibt's einen wunderbaren Klang
Durch den Garten die ganze Nacht.

Die Nachtblume

Nacht ist wie ein stilles Meer,
Lust und Leid und Liebesklagen
Kommen so verworren her
In dem linden Wellenschlagen.

Wünsche wie die Wolken sind,
Schiffen durch die stillen Räume,
Wer erkennt im lauen Wind,
Obs Gedanken oder Träume?—

Schließ ich nun auch Herz und Mund,
Die so gern den Sternen klagen:
Leise doch im Herzensgrund
Bleibt das linde Wellenschlagen.

The fountain babbles its lullaby:
What olden fair days did,
A slumbering lady sits near by,
Her robe in tresses hid.

In her hand she holds a mandolin,
Dreaming she seems to speak.
Did I know her in times already dim? . . .
Hush, tiptoe by, she must not wake.

When night tucks in the valley, then
Her fingers touch the strings,
And, through the garden, through the glen
A wondrous music rings.

Werner Heider (slightly revised)

Night

Night is like a silent sea,
Joy and pain and love's sad urging
Reach us so confusedly
Through the wavelets' gentle surging.

Wishes like light clouds afloat,
Through the quiet spaces drifting,
In this soft wind who can note
If they're thoughts or dream-wraiths shifting?

If I silence voice and heart,
Which would cry out vainly urging
To the stars, still deep apart
Sounds the wavelet's gentle surging.

Isabel S. MacInnes

Waldgespräch

Es ist schon spät, es wird schon kalt,
Was reit'st du einsam durch den Wald?
Der Wald ist lang, du bist allein,
Du schöne Braut! Ich führ' dich heim!

„Groß ist der Männer Trug und List,
Vor Schmerz mein Herz gebrochen ist,
Wohl irrt das Waldhorn her und hin,
O flieh! Du weißt nicht, wer ich bin."

So reich geschmückt ist Roß und Weib,
So wunderschön der junge Leib,
Jetzt kenn' ich dich—Gott steh mir bei!
Du bist die Hexe Lorelei.

„Du kennst mich wohl—von hohem Stein
Schaut still mein Schloß tief in den Rhein.
Es ist schon spät, es wird schon kalt,
Kommst nimmermehr aus diesem Wald!"

Auf meines Kindes Tod

Von fern die Uhren schlagen,
Es ist schon tiefe Nacht,
Die Lampe brennt so düster,
Dein Bettlein ist gemacht.

Die Winde nur noch gehen
Wehklagend um das Haus,
Wir sitzen einsam drinne
Und lauschen oft hinaus.

Conversation in the Forest

The hour is late, the eve grows cold,
Why ride you here alone so bold?
The woodland's wide, I'll be your guide
And lead you home, you lovely bride!

"Man's cunning and deceit are great;
Crushed is my heart beneath grief's weight.
The hunting horn roams to and fro.
O flee! My name you do not know."

Your splendid steed, your dazzling dress,
Your body's young seductiveness—
I know you now! God hear my cry!
You are the sorceress Lorelei!

"You speak the truth—a castle's mine
That towers high above the Rhine.
The hour is late, cold grows the eve,
This forest you shall never leave!"

Gerd Gillhoff

On the Death of my Child

The distant clocks are striking,
It is already late,
The lamp is burning dimly,
Your little bed is made.

Only the winds are whistling
Lamenting past the grounds,
We sit so still and lonely
And listen for your sounds.

Es ist, als müsstest leise
Du klopfen an die Tür,
Du hättst dich nur verirret,
Und kämst nun müd zurück.

Wir armen, armen Toren!
Wir irren ja im Graus
Des Dunkels noch verloren—
Du fandest längst nach Haus.

Memento mori!

Schnapp Austern, Dukaten,
Mußt dennoch sterben!
Dann tafeln die Maden
Und lachen die Erben.

Todeslust

Bevor er in die blaue Flut gesunken,
Träumt noch der Schwan und singet todestrunken;
Die sommermüde Erde im Verblühen
Läßt all ihr Feuer in den Trauben glühen;
Die Sonne, Funken sprühend, im Versinken,
Gibt noch einmal der Erde Glut zu trinken,
Bis, Stern auf Stern, die Trunkne zu empfangen,
Die wunderbare Nacht ist aufgegangen.

It seems as if you gently
Would knock upon the door,
And, though you had been straying,
Would come in tired once more.

We foolish, foolish people!
Confused and lost we roam
In terror of the darkness—
You long ago came home.

Edward Dvoretzky

Memento mori

Eat oysters, hoard ducats
As much as you're able,
You still have to die!
Then the worms come to table
And your heirs can live high.

R. M. Browning

Death Wish

Death-drunk the swan in waters seeks its grave,
To sink still dreaming, singing in the wave;
The summer-wearied earth, when flowers no longer blow,
In clustered grapes sets all her fires aglow;
The sun, still showering sparks throughout the west,
Lends earth his warmth once more before he sets,
Till, star on star, a marvel to behold,
Arises Night, the drunk earth to enfold.

R. M. Browning

Justinus Kerner

Der schwere Traum (Ikaros)

Mir träumt, ich flög gar bange
Weit in die Welt hinaus,
In Strassburg durch alle Gassen
Bis vor Feinsliebchens Haus.

Feinsliebchen! Was hilft lügen,
Da du doch alles weißt!
Wer dich so fliegen lehret,
Das ist der böse Feind.

Feinsliebchen! Was hilft lügen,
Da du doch alles weißt!
Wer mich so fliegen lehrte,
Das ist der böse Geist.

Feinsliebchen weint und schreiet,
Daß ich am Schrei erwacht,
Da lieg' ich, ach! in Augsburg
Gefangen auf der Wacht.

Und morgen muß ich hangen,
Feinslieb mich nicht mehr ruft,
Wohl morgen als ein Vogel
Schweb ich in freier Luft.

Justinus Kerner

Oppressive Dream

I dreamt I flew all fearful
Into the world afar,
To Strassburg through the side-streets,
Before my sweetheart's door.

Sweetheart is so saddened,
My flying makes her cry:
"It was the Evil Spirit
Who taught you how to fly!"

Now Sweetheart, what use lying,
Since you know all full well.
The one who taught me flying,
It was the Fiend from Hell!

And Sweetheart weeps, a-crying
And wakes me with her cry,
And here, alas! in Augsburg
A prisoner I lie.

Tomorrow I'll be hanging,
No Sweetheart calls to me,
Tomorrow I'll be soaring,
A bird in the air and free.

John Fitzell

Ludwig Uhland

Frühlingsglaube

Die linden Lüfte sind erwacht,
Sie säuseln und weben Tag und Nacht,
Sie schaffen an allen Enden.
O frischer Duft, o neuer Klang!
Nun, armes Herze, sei nicht bang!
Nun muß sich alles, alles wenden.

Die Welt wird schöner mit jedem Tag,
Man weiß nicht, was noch werden mag,
Das Blühen will nicht enden.
Es blüht das fernste, tiefste Tal:
Nun, armes Herz, vergiß der Qual!
Nun muß sich alles, alles wenden!

Das Schloß am Meer

„Hast du das Schloß gesehen,
Das hohe Schloß am Meer?
Golden und rosig wehen
Die Wolken drüber her.

„Es möchte sich niederneigen
In die spiegelklare Flut,
Es möchte streben und steigen
In der Abendwolken Glut."—

„Wohl hab ich es gesehen,
Das hohe Schloß am Meer
Und den Mond darüber stehen
Und Nebel weit umher."—

Ludwig Uhland

Spring Faith

The winds again are mild and light;
they whisper and wander day and night,
through field and forest wending.
O fresh perfume, O youthful sound,
now, wretched heart, be thou unbound!
for now must all the world be mending.

The earth grows lovlier day by day;
what yet may be, no one can say:
the blossoming seems unending.
The farthest, deepest valley flowers;
now, heart, forget the painful hours,
for now must all the world be mending.

J. W. Thomas

The Castle by the Sea

"Hast thou seen that lordly castle,
    That castle by the sea?
Golden and red above it
    The clouds float gorgeously.

"And fain it would stoop downward
    To mirrored wave below;
And fain it would soar upward
    In the evening's crimson glow."

"Well have I have seen that castle,
    That castle by the sea,
And the moon above it standing,
    And the mist rise solemnly."

„Der Wind und des Meeres Wallen,
Gaben sie frischen Klang?
Vernahmst du aus hohen Hallen
Saiten und Festgesang?"—

„Die Winde, die Wogen alle
Lagen in tiefer Ruh;
Einem Klagelied aus der Halle
Hört ich mit Tränen zu."—

„Sahest du oben gehen
Den König und sein Gemahl,
Der roten Mäntel Wehen,
Der goldnen Kronen Strahl?

„Führten sie nicht mit Wonne
Eine schöne Jungfrau dar,
Herrlich wie eine Sonne,
Strahlend im goldnen Haar?"—

„Wohl sah ich die Eltern beide,
Ohne der Kronen Licht,
Im schwarzen Trauerkleide—
Die Jungfrau sah ich nicht."

Der gute Kamerad

Ich hatt' einen Kameraden,
Einen bessern findst du nit.
Die Trommel schlug zum Streite,
Er ging an meiner Seite
In gleichem Schritt und Tritt.

Eine Kugel kam geflogen;
Gilt's mir oder gilt es dir?
Ihn hat es weggerissen,

"The winds and the waves of the ocean,
  Had they a merry chime?
Didst thou hear, from those lofty chambers
  The harp and the minstrel's rhyme?"

"The winds and the waves of the ocean,
  They rested quietly,
But I heard on the gale a sound of wail,
  And tears came to mine eye."

"And sawest thou on the turrets
  The King and his royal bride?
And the wave of their crimson mantles?
  And the golden crown of pride?

"Led they not forth, in rapture,
  A beauteous maiden there?
Resplendent as the morning sun,
  Beaming with golden hair?"

"Well saw I the ancient parents,
  Without the crown of pride;
They were moving slow, in weeds of woe,
  No maiden was by their side!"

Henry Wadsworth Longfellow

The Good Comrade

I had a faithful comrade,
None better could you find.
The battle drum beat gaily,
He marched beside me daily,
And never fell behind.

A musket-ball came flying—
Is it meant for me or thee?
It threw him down, and dying

Er liegt mir vor den Füßen,
Als wär's ein Stück von mir.

Will mir die Hand noch reichen,
Derweil ich eben lad:
Kann dir die Hand nicht geben;
Bleib du im ew'gen Leben
Mein guter Kamerad!

Der Wirtin Töchterlein

Es zogen drei Bursche wohl über den Rhein,
Bei einer Frau Wirtin, da kehrten sie ein:

„Frau Wirtin, hat Sie gut Bier und Wein?
Wo hat Sie Ihr schönes Töchterlein?"—

„Mein Bier und Wein ist frisch und klar,
Mein Töchterlein liegt auf der Totenbahr."

Und als sie traten zur Kammer hinein,
Da lag sie in einem schwarzen Schrein.

Der erste, der schlug den Schleier zurück
Und schaute sie an mit traurigem Blick:

„Ach, lebtest du noch, du schöne Maid!
Ich würde dich lieben von dieser Zeit."

Der zweite deckte den Schleier zu
Und kehrte sich ab und weinte dazu:

Before my feet he's lying,
Just like a part of me.

His hand he wants to give me,
While I must load anew;
I cannot give my hand now—
Farewell—in heaven's bright land now,
My comrade good and true!

Margarete Münsterberg and
Charles T. Brooks

The Hostess' Daughter

Three fellows were marching over the Rhine,
They stopped where they saw the hostess' sign.

"Dear hostess, have you good beer and wine?
And where have you your daughter so fair and fine?"

"My beer is good, my wine is clear,
My daughter is lying upon her bier."

Now into the chamber she led the way,
There in a black coffin the maiden lay.

The first man drew the veil aside,
And full of sorrow the maid espied.

"Ah, beautiful maiden, if thou couldst live!
To thee alone my love I would give!"

The second laid back the veil again,
And turned away and wept in pain.

„Ach, daß du liegst auf der Totenbahr!
Ich hab dich geliebet so manches Jahr."

Der dritte hub ihn wieder sogleich
Und küßte sie an den Mund so bleich:

„Dich lieb ich immer, dich lieb ich noch heut
Und werde dich lieben in Ewigkeit."

Friedrich Rückert

Barbarossa

Der alte Barbarossa,
Der Kaiser Friederich,
Im unterird'schen Schlosse
Hält er verzaubert sich.

Er ist niemals gestorben,
Er lebt darin noch jetzt;
Er hat im Schloß verborgen
Zum Schlaf sich hingesetzt.

Er hat hinabgenommen
Des Reiches Herrlichkeit
Und wird einst wiederkommen
Mit ihr zu seiner Zeit.

Der Stuhl ist elfenbeinern,
Darauf der Kaiser sitzt;
Der Tisch ist marmelsteinern,
Worauf sein Haupt er stützt.

"Oh, why must thou lie upon thy bier!
Alas, I have loved thee for many a year."

The third man lifted again the veil,
And kissed her upon her lips so pale:

"I loved thee always, I love thee today,
And I will love thee forever and aye."

Margarete Münsterberg

Friedrich Rückert

Barbarossa

Old Friedrich Barbarossa,
the emperor renowned,
inhabits now, enchanted,
a castle underground.

Not dead is he, but resting,
he still lives there today,
and in this hidden castle
he sits and sleeps away.

He took the empire's glory
down with him in its prime,
and will return in splendor
with it, in his own time.

The chair on which he slumbers
of ivory is made,
the table is of marble
on which his head is laid.

Sein Bart ist nicht von Flachse,
Er ist von Feuersglut,
Ist durch den Tisch gewachsen,
Worauf sein Kinn ausruht.

Er nickt als wie im Traume,
Sein Aug halb offen zwinkt;
Und je nach langem Raume
Er einem Knaben winkt.

Er spricht im Schlaf zum Knaben:
"Geh hin vors Schloß, o Zwerg,
Und sieh, ob noch die Raben
Herfliegen um den Berg.

Und wenn die alten Raben
Noch fliegen immerdar,
So muß ich auch noch schlafen
Verzaubert hundert Jahr."

Wilhelm Müller

Der Lindenbaum

Am Brunnen vor dem Tore,
Da steht ein Lindenbaum;
Ich träumt in seinem Schatten
So manchen süßen Traum.

Ich schnitt in seine Rinde
So manches liebe Wort;
Es zog in Freud und Leide
Zu ihm mich immer fort.

His flowing beard, not flaxen,
but red with fiery glow,
has grown right through the table
and to the stone below.

He nods and stirs in dreaming
and winks a sleepy eye,
and now and then he beckons
a servant, standing by.

He speaks to him in slumber:
"Find out, O dwarf, if still
you see the ravens flying
above the castle hill.

And if the ancient ravens
above the castle soar,
I still must sleep, enchanted,
a hundred years or more."

J. W. Thomas

Wilhelm Müller

The Linden Tree

Before the gateway fountain
there stands a linden tree.
Within its shadows dreaming,
such sweet dreams came to me.

I cut into its gray bark
so many a loving name—
and here in joy and sorrow
is where I always came.

Ich mußt auch heute wandern
Vorbei in tiefer Nacht,
Da hab ich noch im Dunkel
Die Augen zugemacht.

Und seine Zweige rauschten,
Als riefen sie mir zu:
Komm her zu mir, Geselle,
Hier findst du deine Ruh!

Die kalten Winde bliesen
Mir grad ins Angesicht,
Der Hut flog mir vom Kopfe,
Ich wendete mich nicht.

Nun bin ich manche Stunde
Entfernt von jenem Ort,
Und immer hör ich's rauschen:
Du fändest Ruhe dort!

Wanderschaft

Das Wandern ist des Müllers Lust,
Das Wandern!
Das muß ein schlechter Müller sein,
Dem niemals fiel das Wandern ein,
Das Wandern!

Vom Wasser haben wir's gelernt,
Vom Wasser!
Das hat nicht Rast bei Tag und Nacht,
Ist stets auf Wanderschaft bedacht,
Das Wasser!

Das sehn wir auch den Rädern ab,
Den Rädern!

Today I had to wander
right by when night was deep.
Just there once more in darkness
I closed my eyes in sleep.

And all its branches rustled,
the leaves called wistfully:
Come here to me, dear fellow,
you'll find your peace with me.

Cold blasts of wind blew sharply,
cut straight into my face.
My hat flew from my head too—
I never changed my pace.

And now the miles are many
I've wandered without cease,
And still I hear the rustling:
'Tis there that you'd find peace!

John Fitzell

The Journeyman's Song

Oh wandering is a miller's joy,
Oh wandering!
A sorry miller he must be
Who never wanted to be free
For wandering!

The water taught us what to do,
The water!
For it rests not by night or day,
And always strains to be away,
The water!

We learn it from the millwheels too,
The millwheels!

Die gar nicht gerne stille stehn,
Die sich mein Tag nicht müde drehn.
Die Räder!

Die Steine selbst, so schwer sie sind,
Die Steine!
Sie tanzen mit den muntern Reihn
Und wollen gar noch schneller sein,
Die Steine!

O Wandern, Wandern, meine Lust,
O Wandern!
Herr Meister und Frau Meisterin,
Laßt mich in Friede weiter ziehn
Und wandern!

August Graf von Platen-Hallermünde

Tristan

Wer die Schönheit angeschaut mit Augen,
Ist dem Tode schon anheimgegeben,
Wird für keinen Dienst auf Erden taugen,
Und doch wird er vor dem Tode beben,
Wer die Schönheit angeschaut mit Augen!

Ewig währt für ihn der Schmerz der Liebe,
Denn ein Tor nur kann auf Erden hoffen,
Zu genügen einem solchen Triebe:
Wen der Pfeil des Schönen je getroffen,
Ewig währt für ihn der Schmerz der Liebe!

Ach, er möchte wie ein Quell versiechen,
Jedem Hauch der Luft ein Gift entsaugen

They're like the water down below,
I've never seen them weary grow,
The millwheels!

The millstones too, though heavy they,
The millstones!
In merry circles round they dance,
Would like to faster race and prance,
The millstones!

Oh wandering, wandering, my delight,
Oh wandering!
Oh master, mistress miller, pray
Let me in peace now go my way
And wander!

Francis Owen

August Graf von Platen-Hallermünde

Tristan

Whoever has gazed at beauty eye to eye
Is given over, signed and sealed, to death,
Is useless here while drawing earthly breath
Though he may tremble while he fears to die,—
Whoever has gazed at beauty eye to eye!

For him the pain of love endures always
Since only fools can hope, as men alive,
To satisfy, to equal such a drive:
Whom beauty's arrow pierced in earthly days
For him the pain of love endures always.

Oh, he would like to dry up like a spring,
From every breeze suck poison and so die,

Und den Tod aus jeder Blume riechen:
Wer die Schönheit angeschaut mit Augen,
Ach, er möchte wie ein Quell versiechen!

Wie rafft' ich mich auf in der Nacht, in der Nacht,
Und fühlte mich fürder gezogen,
Die Gassen verließ ich, vom Wächter bewacht,
Durchwandelte sacht
In der Nacht, in der Nacht,
Das Tor mit dem gotischen Bogen.

Der Mühlbach rauschte durch felsigen Schacht,
Ich lehnte mich über die Brücke,
Tief unter mir nahm ich der Wogen in acht,
Die wallten so sacht
In der Nacht, in der Nacht,
Doch wallte nicht eine zurücke.

Es drehte sich oben, unzählig entfacht,
Melodischer Wandel der Sterne,
Mit ihnen der Mond in beruhigter Pracht,
Sie funkelten sacht
In der Nacht, in der Nacht,
Durch täuschend entlegene Ferne.

Ich blickte hinauf in der Nacht, in der Nacht,
Ich blickte hinunter aufs neue:
O wehe, wie hast du die Tage verbracht!
Nun stille du sacht
In der Nacht, in der Nacht,
Im pochenden Herzen die Reue!

And smell the smell of death in every thing:
Whoever has gazed at beauty eye to eye,
Oh, he would like to dry up like a spring!

Herman Salinger

Remorse

How I started up in the night, in the night,
   Drawn on without rest or reprieval!
The streets, with their watchmen, were lost to my sight,
   As I wandered so light
   In the night, in the night,
Through the gate with the arch mediaeval.

The mill-brook rushed from the rocky height,
   I leaned o'er the bridge in my yearning;
Deep under me watched I the waves in their flight,
   As they glided so light
   In the night, in the night,
Yet backward not one was returning.

O'erhead were revolving, so countless and bright,
   The stars in melodious existence;
And with them the moon, more serenely bedight;
   They sparkled so light
   In the night, in the night,
Through the magical, measureless distance.

And upward I gazed in the night, in the night,
   And again on the waves in their fleeting;
Ah woe! thou hast wasted thy days in delight,
   Now silence thou light,
   In the night, in the night,
The remorse in my heart that is beating.

Henry Wadsworth Longfellow

Venedig liegt nur noch im Land der Träume
Und wirft nur Schatten her aus alten Tagen,
Es liegt der Leu der Republik erschlagen,
Und öde feiern seines Kerkers Räume.

Die eh'rnen Hengste, die durch salz'ge Schäume
Dahergeschleppt, auf jener Kirche ragen,
Nicht mehr dieselben sind sie, ach! sie tragen
Des korsikan'schen Überwinders Zäume.

Wo ist das Volk von Königen geblieben,
Das diese Marmorhäuser durfte bauen,
Die nun verfallen und gemach zerstieben?

Nur selten finden auf des Enkels Brauen
Der Ahnen große Züge sich geschrieben,
An Dogengräbern in den Stein gehauen.

Der Pilgrim vor St. Just

Nacht ist's und Stürme sausen für und für,
Hispanische Mönche, schließt mir auf die Tür!

Laßt mich hier ruhn, bis Glockenton mich weckt,
Der zum Gebet euch in die Kirche schreckt!

Bereitet mir was euer Haus vermag,
Ein Ordenskleid und einen Sarkophag!

Gönnt mir die kleine Zelle, weiht mich ein,
Mehr als die Hälfte dieser Welt war mein.

Venice, mere shadow of her elder day,
In land of dreams alone lies fresh and fair.
Where frowned the proud Republic's lion, there
His idle prisons now keep holiday.

Those brazen steeds that, hauled through briny spray,
On yonder church-walls shake their streaming hair,
They are the same no longer! Ah, they wear
The bridle of the Corsican Conqueror's sway!

Where is the people gone, the kingly race
That reared these marble piles amid the waves,
Which now decay and fall to dust apace?

Not on the brows of these degenerate slaves
Think thou the traits of their great sires to trace:
Go, read them, hewn in stone, on Doges' graves!

Charles T. Brooks, rev. by R. M. Browning

The Pilgrim at St. Yuste*

Night falls, the wild winds whistle more and more.
O Spanish monks, for me unbar your door!

Here let me rest and waken to the chime
That hurries you to church at praying time.

What your house offers, that I must assume;
Show me a monk's habit and a monk's tomb.

Accept me, set me in a little cell.
Before me more than half the world once fell.

* The Emperor Charles V.

Das Haupt, das nun der Schere sich bequemt,
Mit mancher Krone ward's bediademt.

Die Schulter, die der Kutte nun sich bückt,
Hat kaiserlicher Hermelin geschmückt.

Nun bin ich vor dem Tod den Toten gleich,
Und fall in Trümmer, wie das alte Reich.

Annette von Droste-Hülshoff

Der Weiher

Er liegt so still im Morgenlicht,
So friedlich, wie ein fromm Gewissen;
Wenn Weste seinen Spiegel küssen,
Des Ufers Blume fühlt es nicht;
Libellen zittern über ihn,
Blaugoldne Stäbchen und Karmin,
Und auf des Sonnenbildes Glanz
Die Wasserspinne führt den Tanz;
Schwertlilienkranz am Ufer steht
Und horcht des Schilfes Schlummerliede;
Ein lindes Säuseln kommt und geht,
Als flüstre's: Friede! Friede! Friede!—

Die Mergelgrube

Stoß deinen Scheit drei Spannen in den Sand,
Gesteine siehst du aus dem Schnitte ragen,
Blau, gelb, zinnoberrot, als ob zur Gant

The head that now seeks tonsure and bows down
Was diademed with more than one proud crown.

The shoulder that a cowl has humbled here
Knew ermine and imperial tiring gear.

Not dead, but as the dead, I fall and crack
Like the old Empire crumbling at my back.

Edwin Morgan

Annette von Droste-Hülshoff

The Pond

So still the pond in morning's gray,
A quiet conscience is not clearer.
When west winds kiss its glassy mirror,
The sedges do not feel it sway.
Above it throbs the dragonfly;
Blue-gold and crimson cross and ply.
And where the sun reflected glances,
The water spider skips and dances.
On the bank a lilied ring scarce blows;
The reedy lullaby will not cease.
A rippling rustle comes and goes,
As though it whispered: peace, peace, peace.

Herman Salinger

The Marl-pit

Just thrust your spade three spans into the sand—
Within the cut you see stones, yellow, blue,
And cinnabar, crop up—a kind of stand

Natur die Trödelbude aufgeschlagen.
Kein Pardelfell war je so bunt gefleckt,
Kein Rebhuhn, keine Wachtel so gescheckt,
Als das Gerölle, gleißend wie vom Schliff,
Sich aus der Scholle bröckelt bei dem Griff
Der Hand, dem Scharren mit des Fußes Spitze.
Wie zürnend sturt dich an der schwarze Gneis,
Spatkugeln kollern nieder, milchig weiß,
Und um den Glimmer fahren Silberblitze;
Gesprenkelte Porphyre, groß und klein,
Die Ockerdruse und der Feuerstein—
Nur wenige hat dieser Grund gezeugt,
Der sah den Strand, und der des Berges Kuppe;
Die zorn'ge Welle hat sie hergescheucht,
Leviathan mit seiner Riesenschuppe,
Als schäumend übern Sinai er fuhr,
Des Himmels Schleusen dreißig Tage offen,
Gebirge schmolzen ein wie Zuckerkand,
Als dann am Ararat die Arche stand,
Und eine fremde, üppige Natur,
Ein neues Leben quoll aus neuen Stoffen.—

Findlinge nennt man sie, weil von der Brust,
Der mütterlichen, sie gerissen sind,
In fremde Wiege, schlummernd unbewußt,
Die fremde Hand sie legt' wie's Findelkind.
O welch ein Waisenhaus ist diese Heide,
Die Mohren, Blaßgesicht und rote Haut
Gleichförmig hüllet mit dem braunen Kleide!
Wie endlos ihre Zellenreihn gebaut!

Tief ins Gebröckel, in die Mergelgrube
War ich gestiegen, denn der Wind zog scharf;
Dort saß ich seitwärts in der Höhlenstube
Und horchte träumend auf der Luft Geharf.
Es waren Klänge, wie wenn Geisterhall
Melodisch schwinde im zerstörten All;
Und dann ein Zischen, wie von Moores Klaffen,
Wenn brodelnd es in sich zusamm'gesunken;

Where peddlar Nature's wares are put on view.
Never was dappled leopard-skin this gay,
Or quail or partridge checkered in the way
These pebbles are, ground to a shine; the clod
Releases them to grasp of hand or prod
Of toe-tip. As if raging, black gneiss gazes
Up at you, spar cascades in pellets, white
As milk, and round the mica silver-bright
Trailways of lightning go; the speckled phases
Of porphyries, both big and little; flint
And ocher-druse; a procreative stint
By earth here means that few are local; one
Beheld the shore, and one the mountain's dome;
Scared hither by the angry wave, undone
When over Sinai in a rush of foam
Scaly Leviathan, the monster, surged;
For thirty days the heav'nly sluices parted,
Whole mountain chains dissolved like candy, till
Upon the side of Ararat the Ark stood still,
And out of new materials emerged
A Nature strange and rank, life newly started.

Erratics they are called because they've strayed,
Torn by strange hands from the maternal breast
While slumbering unconscious, to be laid
Into strange cradles, for a foundling's rest.
This heath—o what an orphanage! The gown
Is uniform, for every one's subjected—
Black, paleface, redskin—to a common brown!
Their cells stretch on, in endless rows erected!

The wind was biting, so I had descended
Into the deep scree of the marl-pit; there
I sat, lodged sideways in the cave; attended,
If dreamily, to harp-sounds from the air,
A ringing as when spirit-tones disperse,
Still tuneful, in a ruined universe;
And then a hissing, as when through a gaping
In peat that's settling there's an ebullition;

Mir überm Haupt ein Rispeln und ein Schaffen,
Als scharre in der Asche man den Funken.
Findlinge zog ich Stück auf Stück hervor
Und lauschte, lauschte mit berauschtem Ohr.

Vor mir, um mich der graue Mergel nur;
Was drüber, sah ich nicht; doch die Natur
Schien mir verödet, und ein Bild erstand
Von einer Erde, mürbe, ausgebrannt;
Ich selber schien ein Funken mir, der doch
Erzittert in der toten Asche noch,
Ein Findling im zerfallnen Weltenbau.
Die Wolke teilte sich, der Wind ward lau;
Mein Haupt nicht wagt' ich aus dem Hohl zu strecken,
Um nicht zu schauen der Verödung Schrecken,
Wie Neues quoll und Altes sich zersetzte—
War ich der erste Mensch oder der letzte?

Ha, auf der Schieferplatte hier Medusen—
Noch schienen ihre Strahlen sie zu zücken,
Als sie geschleudert von des Meeres Busen
Und das Gebirge sank, sie zu zerdrücken.
Es ist gewiß, die alte Welt ist hin,
Ich Petrefakt, ein Mammutsknochen drin!
Und müde, müde sank ich an den Rand
Der staub'gen Gruft; da rieselte der Grand
Auf Haar und Kleider mir, ich ward so grau
Wie eine Leich' im Katakomben-Bau,
Und mir zu Füßen hört' ich leises Knirren,
Ein Rütteln, ein Gebröckel und ein Schwirren.
Es war der Totenkäfer, der im Sarg
Soeben eine frische Leiche barg;
Ihr Fuß, ihr Flügelchen empor gestellt
Zeigt eine Wespe mir von dieser Welt.
Und anders ward mein Träumen nun gewandet,
Zu einer Mumie ward ich versandet,
Mein Linnen Staub, fahlgrau mein Angesicht,
Und auch der Skarabäus fehlte nicht.

Above my head a swish and active scraping
As in the ashes for a spark's emission.
I listened, my ear drunk, and to release
Them, pulled erratics forth, piece after piece.

Before me, round me only marl, that gray;
I did not see above, but felt decay
As Nature's mark; a picture came to me
Of earth burnt out and crumbling; I could see
Myself: a spark that trembled still amid
Dead ash; cosmic disintegration hid
This lost erratic. As the clouds grew thin,
The wind turned milder; but for me, within
The hole, to stick my head out was too daring,
Lest I would be, in desolation, staring
At horror, with new flowing, old dissolving:
Was I the last man—or the first, evolving?

Ah, on the schist-plate here, medusae—wielding
Their rays still, so it seemed, amidst that rushing,
Flung from the bosom of the sea, just yielding,
While mountains sank, to the oppressive crushing.
Surely the world of old is past: it's been,
A fossil I—a mammoth's bone therein!
So tired, so tired, I sank on the edge there
Beside the powd'ry grave; onto my hair
And clothes grit trickled, till I grayed like some
Corpse in the catacombs; and I heard come
Up from my feet a gentle grinding, whirring,
Shaking: a sexton beetle'd been interring
A fresh corpse in its coffin; lifted high,
A wasp's small wing, its foot could testify
For me to such a world. And now it changed,
My dreaming, its direction rearranged:
Sanded all over, I had been transmuted
Into a mummy, dust now constituted
My linens, gray my countenance and pale,
Nor was the scarabaeus far to hail.

Wie, Leichen über mir?—so eben gar
Rollt mir ein Byssusknäuel in den Schoß;
Nein, das ist Wolle, ehrlich Lämmerhaar—
Und plötzlich ließen mich die Träume los.
Ich gähnte, dehnte mich, fuhr aus dem Hohl,
Am Himmel stand der rote Sonnenball,
Getrübt von Dunst, ein glüher Karneol,
Und Schafe weideten am Heidewall.
Dicht über mir sah ich den Hirten sitzen,
Er schlingt den Faden, und die Nadeln blitzen,
Wie er bedächtig seinen Socken strickt.
Zu mir hinunter hat er nicht geblickt.
„Ave Maria" hebt er an zu pfeifen,
So sacht und schläfrig, wie die Lüfte streifen.
Er schaut so seelengleich die Herde an,
Daß man nicht weiß, ob Schaf er oder Mann.
Ein Räuspern dann, und langsam aus der Kehle
Schiebt den Gesang er in das Garngesträhle:

„Es stehet ein Fischlein in einem tiefen See,
Danach tu ich wohl schauen, ob es kommt in die Höh';
Wandl' ich über Grunheide bis an den kühlen Rhein,
Alle meine Gedanken bei meinem Feinsliebchen sein.

Gleich wie der Mond ins Wasser schaut hinein,
Und gleich wie die Sonne im Wald gibt güldenen Schein,
Also sich verborgen bei mir die Liebe findt,
Alle meine Gedanken, sie sind bei dir, mein Kind.

Wer da hat gesagt, ich wollte wandern fort,
Der hat sein Feinsliebchen an einem andern Ort;
Trau nicht den falschen Zungen, was sie dir blasen ein,
Alle meine Gedanken, sie sind bei dir allein."

Ich war hinaufgeklommen, stand am Bord,
Dicht vor dem Schäfer, reichte ihm den Knäuel;
Er steckt' ihn an den Hut und strickte fort,
Sein weißer Kittel zuckte wie ein Weihel.
Im Moose lag ein Buch; ich hob es auf—

What—corpses over me? Into my lap
There rolls just now a noil of byssus; no,
It's honest lamb's-wool from the fleece, a scrap—
And suddenly my dreams all let me go.
I yawned and stretched and left the cave; a ball,
The sun hung in the sky, filtered through haze,
A glow of red carnelian; by the wall,
The levee in the moor, I saw sheep graze,
And right up over me the shepherd sitting;
He casts on, needles flashing: he is knitting
His sock deliberatively. His eye
Has not strayed down to me. He has a try
At whistling a "Hail Mary," with an easy
Softness and drowsiness as from a breezy
Caress. He views his flock with kinship; deep
At heart (one asks) is he a man or sheep?
And then he clears his throat, slowly consigning
To carded yarn his song, a close entwining:

"A little fish in a deep, deep lake has its stop,
I'd better look and see if it's coming to the top;
Wand'ring over Grunheide's far as the cool Rhine,
All the thoughts I have are with that little darling of mine.

Just as the moon looks in the water below,
And just as the sun in the woods shines with golden glow,
So love is found hidden away in me inside,
All the thoughts I have are with you, dear girl, and abide.

The one who said that I was wanting to stray,
He's got his little darling somewhere far away;
Don't trust the lying tongues, what they whisper you's untrue,
All the thoughts I have, they're with you alone, with you."

I'd climbed up to the rim, stood right before
The shepherd, holding out the noil. He, taking
It, stuck it on his hat; went back to more
Knitting, from which his white smock frock was shaking
As might a nun's veil. From the moss I picked

„Bertuchs Naturgeschichte; lest Ihr das?"
Da zog ein Lächeln seine Lippen auf:
„Der lügt mal, Herr! Doch das ist just der Spaß!
Von Schlangen, Bären, die in Stein verwandelt,
Als, wie Genesis sagt, die Schleusen offen;
Wär's nicht zur Kurzweil, wär' es schlecht gehandelt:
Man weiß ja doch, daß alles Vieh versoffen."
Ich reichte ihm die Schieferplatte: „Schau,
Das war ein Tier." Da zwinkert' er die Brau
Und hat mir lange pfiffig nachgelacht—
Daß ich verrückt sei, hätt' er nicht gedacht!—

Im Grase

Süße Ruh', süßer Taumel im Gras,
Von des Krautes Arome umhaucht,
Tiefe Flut, tief tief trunkne Flut,
Wenn die Wolk' am Azure verraucht,
Wenn aufs müde, schwimmende Haupt
Süßes Lachen gaukelt herab,
Liebe Stimme säuselt und träuft
Wie die Lindenblüt' auf ein Grab.

Wenn im Busen die Toten dann,
Jede Leiche sich streckt und regt,
Leise, leise den Odem zieht,
Die geschloßne Wimper bewegt,
Tote Lieb', tote Lust, tote Zeit,
All die Schätze, im Schutt verwühlt,
Sich berühren mit schüchternem Klang
Gleich den Glöckchen, vom Winde umspielt.

Stunden, flüchtger ihr als der Kuß
Eines Strahls auf den trauernden See,
Als des ziehenden Vogels Lied,
Das mir nieder perlt aus der Höh',

A book up—"History of Nature by
Bertuch; you're reading that?" Smiling, he flicked
His lips up: "What he says, sir, is a lie.
Some joke! He has the snakes and bears all turning
To stone, while Genesis's sluices flow!
If 'tweren't in fun, a business for unlearning:
The Flood swamped all the beasts, I'll have you know!"
I handed him the schist-plate: "This, you see,
Was once an animal." I left, while he,
Arching his brow—he'd not supposed that I
Was mad—, kept laughing at me on the sly!—

Joseph B. Dallett

In the Grass

Sweet repose, rapture sweet in the grass
With the scent of the herbs around you
Deep surge, deep surge of ecstasy
When the cloud dissolves in the blue
When sweet laughter comes fluttering down
On your weary and swimming head,
A dear voice whispers, drifting to earth
Like lime-blooms on the grave of the dead.

When the dead in your breast then move
Each corpse stretches gently and waits,
Gently draws its breath and breathes out,
Its closed eyelashes gently vibrates,
Buried love, buried joy, buried time,
Treasures dead in the dust, all these
Touch each other with hesitant note,
Little bells played upon by the breeze.

Hours, more fleeting you are than the kiss
Of the sun on the mourning lake,
Than the song of the bird in flight
Pearling down to me in the brake;

Als des schillernden Käfers Blitz,
Wenn den Sonnenpfad er durcheilt,
Als der heiße Druck einer Hand,
Die zum letzten Male verweilt.

Dennoch, Himmel, immer mir nur
Dieses Eine mir: für das Lied
Jedes freien Vogels im Blau
Eine Seele, die mit ihm zieht,
Nur für jeden kärglichen Strahl
Meinen farbig schillernden Saum,
Jeder warmen Hand meinen Druck,
Und für jedes Glück meinen Traum.

Heinrich Heine

Ein Fichtenbaum steht einsam
Im Norden auf kahler Höh'.
Ihn schläfert; mit weißer Decke
Umhüllen ihn Eis und Schnee.

Er träumt von eine Palme,
Die fern im Morgenland
Einsam und schweigend trauert
Auf brennender Felsenwand.

Wenn ich an deinem Hause
Des Morgens vorübergeh',
So freut's mich, du liebe Kleine,
Wenn ich dich am Fenster seh'.

Than the beetle's glitter and flash
As he crosses the sunlit space,
Than the pressure warm of a hand
In a lingering last embrace.

Heaven grant me this one desire,
This alone: for each free bird's song
As it flies in the sky above,
Just one soul which may travel along;
And for each meagre ray of the sun
My own bright iridescent seam,
For each warm hand the clasp of mine,
For each happiness just a dream.

Ursula Prideaux

Heinrich Heine

A spruce is standing lonely
in the North on a barren height.
He drowses; ice and snowflakes
wrap him in a blanket of white.

He dreams about a palm tree
in a distant, eastern land,
that languishes lonely and silent
upon the scorching sand.

Max Knight

When I go past your window
Each shining morning, then
My heart is glad, dear little one,
To see you there again.

Mit deinen schwarzbraunen Augen
Siehst du mich forschend an:
"Wer bist du, und was fehlt dir,
Du fremder, kranker Mann?"—

„Ich bin ein deutscher Dichter,
Bekannt im deutschen Land;
Nennt man die besten Namen,
So wird auch der meine genannt.

„Und was mir fehlt, du Kleine,
Fehlt manchem im deutschen Land;
Nennt man die schlimmsten Schmerzen,
So wird auch der meine genannt."

Ich wollte, meine Lieder
Das wären Blümelein:
Ich schickte sie zu riechen
Der Herzallerliebsten mein.

Ich wollte, meine Lieder
Das wären Küsse fein:
Ich schickt' sie heimlich alle
Nach Liebchens Wängelein.

Ich wollte, meine Lieder
Das wären Erbsen klein:
Ich kocht' eine Erbsensuppe,
Die sollte köstlich sein.

Mir träumte wieder der alte Traum:
Es war eine Nacht im Maie,
Wir saßen unter dem Lindenbaum
Und schwuren uns ewige Treue.

Your dark brown eyes look questions
And seem as if to speak:
"Who are you, and what ails you
Who look so strange and bleak?"

—"I am a German poet,
In Germany well known,
Name the greatest names and
You're sure to name my own.

"And that which ails me, little one,
Makes many Germans moan;
Name the greatest sorrows—
You're sure to name my own."

Hal Draper

I wish that all my love-songs
   Were flowers bright and rare;
I'd send them to my dearest
   And she might find them fair.

I wish that all my love-songs
   Were kisses that could speak;
I'd send them to my dearest
   To hang about her cheek.

I wish that these, my love-songs,
   Were peas, so firm and fat;
I'd make a nice, rich pea-soup—
   And she would relish *that!*

Louis Untermeyer

I dreamt the old, old dream anew:
It was a night in May;
Under the linden we swore to be true
Forever and a day.

Das war ein Schwören und Schwören aufs neu',
Ein Kichern, ein Kosen, ein Küssen;
Daß ich gedenk des Schwures sei,
Hast du in die Hand mich gebissen.

O Liebchen mit den Äuglein klar!
O Liebchen schön und bissig!
Das Schwören in der Ordnung war,
Das Beißen war überflüssig.

Die Lotusblume ängstigt
Sich vor der Sonne Pracht,
Und mit gesenktem Haupte
Erwartet sie träumend die Nacht.

Der Mond, der ist ihr Buhle,
Er weckt sie mit seinem Licht,
Und ihm entschleiert sie freundlich
Ihr frommes Blumengesicht.

Sie blüht und glüht und leuchtet
Und starret stumm in die Höh';
Sie duftet und weinet und zittert
Vor Liebe und Liebesweh.

Aus alten Märchen winkt es
Hervor mit weißer Hand,
Da singt es und da klingt es
Von einem Zauberland:

Wo große Blumen schmachten
Im goldnen Abendlicht
Und zärtlich sich betrachten
Mit bräutlichem Gesicht;—

What swearing and swearing and swearing some more,
How kisses our passion fanned!
So that I shouldn't forget what I swore,
You bit me in the hand.

O mordant love with eyes of light!
O stars of love that light me!
That swearing business was all right,
But you didn't need to bite me.

Herman Salinger

The lotus flower is drooping
In the sun's majestic light;
With lowered languid forehead
Dreaming she waits for the night.

The moon he is her lover;
She wakes in his beams' embrace,
To her lover alone unveiling
The innocent flower of her face.

She beams and gleams and glistens
And gazes mutely above;
She weeps scented tears and trembles
With love and the pain of love.

Hal Draper

From olden tales it flings out
A beckoning white hand;
It sings out and it rings out
From an enchanted land

Where blossoms tall and slender
In gold-lit eventide
Look up with eyes as tender
As the eyes of a loving bride—

Wo alle Bäume sprechen
Und singen, wie ein Chor,
Und laute Quellen brechen
Wie Tanzmusik hervor;—

Und Liebesweisen tönen,
Wie du sie nie gehört,
Bis wundersüßes Sehnen
Dich wundersüß betört!

Ach, könnt' ich dorthin kommen
Und dort mein Herz erfreun
Und aller Qual entnommen
Und frei und selig sein!

Ach! jenes Land der Wonne,
Das seh' ich oft im Traum,
Doch kommt die Morgensonne,
Zerfließt's wie eitel Schaum.

Der Asra

Täglich ging die wunderschöne
Sultanstochter auf und nieder
Um die Abendzeit am Springbrunn,
Wo die weißen Wasser plätschern.

Täglich stand der junge Sklave
Um die Abendzeit am Springbrunn,
Wo die weißen Wasser plätschern;
Täglich ward er bleich und bleicher.

Eines Abends trat die Fürstin
Auf ihn zu mit raschen Worten:
„Deinen Namen will ich wissen,
Deine Heimat, deine Sippschaft!"

Where all the trees have voices
And sing their choral chants,
And every rill rejoices
In music for the dance—

And songs of love are thronging
Such as you never heard
Till hearts with sweetest longing
Are wonder-sweetly stirred!

Ah, could I only go there
And free my heart of pain,
And banish all my woe there,
Be free and blest again!

Ah, land of bliss undying,
I see it oft in dreams.
When dawn comes, it goes flying
Like foam in the morning beams.

Hal Draper

The Asra

Daily came the lone and lovely
Sultan's daughter, slowly wandering
In the evening to the fountain
Where the plashing waters whitened.

Daily stood the youthful captive
In the evening by the fountain
Where the plashing waters whitened—
Daily growing pale and paler.

Till one dusk the strolling princess
Stopped, and suddenly addressed him:
"Tell me now thy name, and tell me
Of thy country and thy kindred."

Und der Sklave sprach: „Ich heiße
Mohamet, ich bin aus Yemmen,
Und mein Stamm sind jene Asra,
Welche sterben, wenn sie lieben."

Helena

Du hast mich beschworen aus dem Grab
Durch deinen Zauberwillen,
Belebtest mich mit Wollustglut—
Jetzt kannst du die Glut nicht stillen.

Press' deinen Mund an meinen Mund,
Der Menschen Odem ist göttlich!
Ich trinke deine Seele aus,
Die Toten sind unersättlich.

Gedächtnisfeier

Keine Messe wird man singen,
Keinen Kadosch wird man sagen,
Nichts gesagt und nichts gesungen
Wird an meinen Sterbetagen.

Doch vielleicht an solchem Tage,
Wenn das Wetter schön und milde,
Geht spazieren auf Montmartre
Mit Paulinen Frau Mathilde.

Mit dem Kranz von Immortellen
Kommt sie, mir das Grab zu schmücken,

And the slave replied, "My name is
Móhamet; I come from Yemen.
And my people are the Asra,
Who, whene'er they love, must perish."

Louis Untermeyer

Helena

Thou hast invoked me from my grave,
   And through thy magic spell
Hast quickened me with fierce desire,
   This flame thou canst not quell.

Oh press thy lips against my lips,
   Divine is mortal breath;
I drink thy very soul from thee.
   Insatiable is death.

Emma Lazarus

Memorial Day

No high mass will they be chanting,
and no *kaddish* * will they say.
Nothing will be said nor chanted
on my own memorial day.

But perhaps on such a morning,
if the air is fresh and clean,
there may stroll on the Montmartre
my Mathilde with Pauline.* *

With a wreath of everlastings
she will come, my grave adorning,

* Jewish prayer for the dead.
* * Companion to Heine's wife, Mathilde.

Und sie seufzet: *Pauvre homme!*
Feuchte Wehmut in den Blicken.

Leider wohn' ich viel zu hoch,
Und ich habe meiner Süßen
Keinen Stuhl hier anzubieten;
Ach! sie schwankt mit müden Füßen.

Süßes, dickes Kind, du darfst
Nicht zu Fuß nach Hause gehen;
An dem Barriere-Gitter
Siehst du die Fiaker stehen.

Ich hatte einst ein schönes Vaterland.
Der Eichenbaum
Wuchs dort so hoch, die Veilchen nickten sanft.
Es war ein Traum.

Das küßte mich auf deutsch und sprach auf deutsch
(Man glaubt es kaum
Wie gut es klang) das Wort: „Ich liebe dich!"
Es war ein Traum.

Nikolaus Lenau

Einsamkeit

I

Hast du schon je dich ganz allein gefunden,
Lieblos und ohne Gott auf einer Heide,
Die Wunden schnöden Mißgeschicks verbunden
Mit stolzer Stille, zornig dumpfem Leide?

sighing softly, "Poor old fellow,"
moist her eye in tearful mourning.

My new home is much too high now;
I can't offer to my dearie
so much as a chair to sit on.
Oh, she sways, her feet are weary.

Walking home, my dear plump darling,
would be much too aggravating.
Look, outside the cemetery,
by the gate, some cabs are waiting.

Max Knight

Oh, once I had a lovely fatherland.
   The oaks grew tall
Up to the sky, the gentle violets swayed.
   I dreamt it all.

I felt a German kiss, heard German words
   (Hard to recall
How good they rang)—the words *Ich liebe dich!*
   I dreamt it all.

Hal Draper

Nikolaus Lenau

Loneliness

I

If ever you have found yourself alone,
Loveless, bereft of God, upon the plain,
And bound your wounds, silent, too proud to groan,
Defying fate to strike you once again;

War jede frohe Hoffnung dir entschwunden,
Wie einem Jäger an der Bergesscheide
Stirbt das Gebell von den verlornen Hunden,
Wie's Vöglein zieht, daß es den Winter meide?

Warst du auf einer Heide so allein,
So weißt du auch, wie's einen dann bezwingt,
Daß er umarmend stürzt an einen Stein;

Daß er, von seiner Einsamkeit erschreckt,
Entsetzt empor vom starren Felsen springt
Und bang dem Winde nach die Arme streckt.

II

Der Wind ist fremd, du kannst ihn nicht umfassen,
Der Stein ist tot, du wirst beim kalten, derben
Umsonst um eine Trosteskunde werben,
So fühlst du auch bei Rosen dich verlassen;

Bald siehst du sie, dein ungewahr, erblassen,
Beschäftigt nur mit ihrem eignen Sterben.
Geh weiter: überall grüßt dich Verderben
In der Geschöpfe langen, dunklen Gassen;

Siehst hier und dort sie aus den Hütten schauen,
Dann schlagen sie vor dir die Fenster zu,
Die Hütten stürzen, und du fühlst ein Grauen.

Lieblos und ohne Gott! der Weg ist schaurig,
Der Zugwind in den Gassen kalt; und du?—
Die ganze Welt ist zum Verzweifeln traurig.

Der Nachtwind hat in den Bäumen
Sein Rauschen eingestellt,
Die Vögel sitzen und träumen
Am Aste traut gesellt.

If ever every happy hope has flown,
As listens to his lost pack's cry in vain
The mountain hunter and hears how far their tone,
As flees the bird from winter's snow and rain;

Were you thus on a lone heath all alone,
You know then too how some force made you kneel
And fling your arms around a silent stone;

And how, frightened by loneliness, you rise
In horror from the rock that cannot feel
And stretch your arms out to the windy skies.

II

The wind is alien; your arms naught enfold;
The stone is dead; from it you seek in vain
A word of comfort that might still your pain;
The gentle roses are no whit less cold;

You see them, unaware of you, unfold—
Busied with their own dying; and again
Where'er you turn decay and death obtain
And all life's highways in their thralldom hold.

And if you see from out their huts men start
They slam the windows shut before your stare;
The huts collapse; stark horror grips your heart.

Loveless, bereft of God, your path is dread;
The wind of life grows cold; your own despair
Fills the whole world and finds it cold and dead.

Winthrop H. Root

The evening wind in the treetops
Has ceased its rustling now,
The birds are sitting and dreaming
Together on the bough.

Die ferne schmächtige Quelle,
Weil alles andre ruht,
Läßt hörbar nun Welle auf Welle
Hinflüstern ihre Flut.

Und wenn die Nähe verklungen,
Dann kommen an die Reih'
Die leisen Erinnerungen
Und weinen fern vorbei.

Daß alles vorübersterbe,
Ist alt und allbekannt;
Doch diese Wehmut, die herbe,
Hat niemand noch gebannt.

Bitte

Weil auf mir, du dunkles Auge,
Übe deine ganze Macht,
Ernste, milde, träumerische,
Unergründlich süße Nacht!

Nimm mit deinem Zauberdunkel
Diese Welt von hinnen mir,
Das du über meinem Leben
Einsam schwebest für und für.

Die Drei

Drei Reiter nach verlorner Schlacht,
Wie reiten sie so sacht, so sacht!

Aus tiefen Wunden quillt das Blut,
Es spürt das Roß die warme Flut.

The distant, trickling streamlet,
Since other sounds are done,
Audibly, wave upon wavelet,
Now lets its waters run.

And when what is near falls silent,
Then come in doleful train
Soft-footed recollections
And, weeping, part again.

That everything dies and passes
Is a truth we all well know,
But of our bitter sadness
None yet has stanched the flow.

R. M. Browning

Plea

Rest upon me, eye of darkness,
Practice now your every might,
Never fathomed in your beauty,
Solemn, gentle, dreaming night.

By the magic of your darkness
Take from me this world away,
That above my life forever
Lonely you may keep your sway.

G. C. Schoolfield

The Three

Three riders after harsh defeat,
How slowly, slowly they retreat!

From deep-cut gashes gushes blood,
The horses feel the unstanched flood.

Vom Sattel tropft das Blut, vom Zaum,
Und spült hinunter Staub und Schaum.

Die Rosse schreiten sanft und weich,
Sonst flöss' das Blut zu rasch, zu weich.

Die Reiter reiten dicht gesellt,
Und einer sich am andern hält.

Sie sehn sich traurig ins Gesicht,
Und einer um den andern spricht:

„Mir blüht daheim die schönste Maid,
Drum tut mein früher Tod mir leid."—

„Hab' Haus und Hof und grünen Wald,
Und sterben muß ich hier so bald!"—

„Den Blick hab' ich in Gottes Welt,
Sonst nichts, doch schwer mir's Sterben fällt."

Und lauernd auf den Todesritt
Ziehn durch die Luft drei Geier mit.

Sie teilen kreischend unter sich:
„Den speisest du, den du, den ich."

Eduard Mörike

Im Frühling

Hier lieg ich auf dem Frühlingshügel:
Die Wolke wird mein Flügel,
Ein Vogel fliegt mir voraus.

From saddle drips the blood, from rein,
And washes foam off flank and mane.

The steeds' advance is gently slow,
For else too swift the blood's rich flow.

The dying horsemen, side by side,
Clasp one another as they ride.

In accents faint, disconsolate,
Each mourns that this should be his fate:

"A maid has promised me her hand—
Why must I die in foreign land?"

"Have home and farm and forest green,
And meet a death so unforeseen!"

"God gave me life, his only boon,
And yet I dread to die so soon."

And where they on their death-ride fare,
Three vultures follow through the air.

They share the men with piercing cry:
"Him you devour, him you, him I!"

Gerd Gillhoff

Eduard Mörike

In Spring

I lie here on the hill of spring;
The cloud becomes my wing;
A bird flies away at my feet.

Ach, sag mir, all-einzige Liebe,
Wo *du* bleibst, daß ich bei dir bliebe!
Doch du und die Lüfte, ihr habt kein Haus.

Der Sonnenblume gleich steht mein Gemüte offen,
Sehnend,
Sich dehnend
In Liebe und Hoffen.
Frühling, was bist du gewillt?
Wann werd ich gestillt?

Die Wolke seh ich wandeln und den Fluß,
Es dringt der Sonne goldner Kuß
Mir tief bis ins Geblüt hinein;
Die Augen, wunderbar berauschet,
Tun, als schliefen sie ein,
Nur noch das Ohr dem Ton der Biene lauschet.
Ich denke dies und denke das,
Ich sehne mich, und weiß nicht recht, nach was:
Halb ist es Lust, halb ist es Klage;
Mein Herz, o sage,
Was webst du für Erinnerung
In golden grüner Zweige Dämmerung?
—Alte unnennbare Tage!

Er ists

Frühling läßt sein blaues Band
Wieder flattern durch die Lüfte;
Süße, wohlbekannte Düfte
Streifen ahnungsvoll das Land.
Veilchen träumen schon,
Wollen balde kommen.
—Horch, von fern ein leiser Harfenton!

Ah tell me, all-singular love,
Where you take rest that with you I may stay;
But you and the breezes, you have no retreat.

My spirit like the sunflower stands wide open,
Yearning,
Out-turning
In loving and hoping.
Spring, what goads you, possessed?
When shall I be at rest?

I watch the motion of the cloud and stream;
The golden kiss of the sunbeam
Into my heart pierces deep;
My eyes, by potent lethargies
Sung shut, might seem asleep,
But the ear catches still the sound of bees.
I think of this and think of that,
I long, and do not rightly know for what,
Half it delights me, half dismays;
Say, heart, O phrase,
What recollection do you weave
Out of dawn mist the gold-green branches leave?
Old, unnamable days!

Vernon Watkins

He Comes

Spring's blue ribbon flutters gaily
Once again upon the air.
Sweet familiar fragrancies
Hover bodeful everywhere.
Violets already dreaming,
Now will soon appear.—
Hark! soft strains of distant music

Frühling, ja du bists!
Dich hab ich vernommen!

An eine Äolsharfe

Tu semper urges flebilibus modis
Mysten ademptum: nec tibi Vespero
Surgente decedunt amores,
Nec rapidum fugiente Solem.

Horaz

Angelehnt an die Efeuwand
Dieser alten Terrasse,
Du, einer luftgebornen Muse
Geheimnisvolles Saitenspiel,
Fang an,
Fange wieder an
Deine melodische Klage!

Ihr kommet, Winde, fern herüber,
Ach! von des Knaben,
Der mir so lieb war,
Frisch grünendem Hügel.
Und Frühlingsblüten unterweges streifend,
Übersättigt mit Wohlgerüchen,
Wie süß bedrängt ihr dies Herz!
Und säuselt her in die Saiten,
Angezogen von wohllautender Wehmut,
Wachsend im Zug meiner Sehnsucht,
Und hinsterbend wieder.

Harp-like reach the ear.
Yes, Spring, it is you!
I knew that you were near.

Geoffrey Herbert Chase

To an Aeolian Harp

> *Tu semper urges flebilibus modis*
> *Mysten ademptum: nec tibi Vespero*
> *Surgente decedunt amores,*
> *Nec rapidum fugiente Solem.* *

Horace

Leaning against the ivy wall
Of this old terrace,
You, instrument mysterious
Of a muse born of the air,
Begin,
And again begin
Your melodious lament.

Winds, you are coming from far,
Ah, from the fresh green
Hill he is under,
The boy I loved so well.
And combing springtime blossoms as you pass,
Drenched with perfumes,
How sweetly you press at my heart,
And whisper among the strings,
Ondrawn by sonorous sorrow's moan,
Rising in the motion of my grief,
And dying away again.

---

* You keep besetting Mystes, who has been taken away, with tearful melodies: your
loves do not leave you when Hesperus rises, nor when it flees before the fast-
moving sun.

Aber auf einmal,
Wie der Wind heftiger herstößt,
Ein holder Schrei der Harfe
Wiederholt, mir zu süßem Erschrecken,
Meiner Seele plötzliche Regung;
Und hier—die volle Rose streut, geschüttelt,
All ihre Blätter vor meine Füße!

Peregrina

I

Der Spiegel dieser treuen, braunen Augen
Ist wie von innerem Gold ein Widerschein;
Tief aus dem Busen scheint er's anzusaugen,
Dort mag solch Gold in heil'gem Gram gedeihn.
In diese Nacht des Blickes mich zu tauchen,
Unwissend Kind, du selber lädst mich ein—
Willst, ich soll kecklich mich und dich entzünden,
Reichst lächelnd mir den Tod im Kelch der Sünden!

II

Aufgeschmückt ist der Freudensaal.
Lichterhell, bunt, in laulicher Sommernacht
Stehet das offene Gartengezelte.
Säulengleich steigen, gepaart,
Grün-umranket, eherne Schlangen,
Zwölf, mit verschlungenen Hälsen,
Tragend und stützend das
Leicht gegitterte Dach.

Aber die Braut noch wartet verborgen
In dem Kämmerlein ihres Hauses.
Endlich bewegt sich der Zug der Hochzeit,
Fackeln tragend,
Feierlich stumm.
Und in der Mitte,

But all at once,
As the wind heaves a heavier sigh,
A tender cry from the harp
Repeats, sweetly startling me,
The sudden tremor through my soul;
And here—the full rose loosens, shaken,
At my feet all its petals.

Christopher Middleton

Peregrina

I

The mirror of these brown and oyal eyes
Is as of inner gold the afterglov ;
Sucked from the heart the splendor seems to rise;
Such gold might flourish there in holy sorrow.
To plunge into this dark night of your gaze
You ask me, child, but this you cannot know;
To set us both on fire with wild beguiling:
Death in the cup of sin you hand me, smiling.

II

The place of joy is adorned for festival.
Glittering with lamps and colors the pavilion
Stands open in the summery night.
Like columns, in pairs,
Green vines over them, serpents of brass,
Twelve, with necks entwined,
Hold and support the
Lightly latticed roof.

But the bride waits, hidden still
At home in her chamber.
At last the wedding procession has begun,
Torches aloft,
In solemn silence.
And in the midst of it walks,

Mich an der rechten Hand,
Schwarz gekleidet, geht einfach die Braut;
Schön gefaltet ein Scharlachtuch
Liegt um den zierlichen Kopf geschlagen.
Lächelnd geht sie dahin; das Mahl schon duftet.

Später im Lärmen des Fests
Stahlen wir seitwärts uns beide
Weg, nach den Schatten des Gartens wandelnd,
Wo im Gebüsche die Rosen brannten,
Wo der Mondstrahl um Lilien zuckte,
Wo die Weymouthsfichte mit schwarzem Haar
Den Spiegel des Teiches halb verhängt.

Auf seidnem Rasen dort, ach, Herz am Herzen,
Wie verschlangen, erstickten meine Küsse den scheueren Kuß!
Indes der Springquell, unteilnehmend
An überschwänglicher Liebe Geflüster,
Sich ewig des eigenen Plätscherns freute;
Uns aber neckten von fern und lockten
Freundliche Stimmen,
Flöten und Saiten umsonst.

Ermüdet lag, zu bald für mein Verlangen,
Das leichte, liebe Haupt auf meinem Schoß.
Spielender Weise mein Aug' auf ihres drückend
Fühlt' ich ein Weilchen die langen Wimpern,
Bis der Schlaf sie stellte,
Wie Schmetterlingsgefieder auf und nieder gehn.

Eh' has Frührot schien,
Eh' das Lämpchen erlosch im Brautgemache,
Weckt' ich die Schläferin,
Führte das seltsame Kind in mein Haus ein.

With me on her right hand,
The bride in simple black;
Around her delicate head in lovely folds
Is looped a cloth of scarlet.
Smiling she walks along; a fragrance
Floats from the banquet.

Later we left the clamor of feasting
And went aside together,
Walking away toward the garden shadows,
Where the roses glowed in the bushes,
Where the moonray flickered around lilies,
Where the weeping pine, with black hair,
Half hid the mirror of the pool.

There on silken turf, ah, heart to heart,
We embraced, my kisses stifling her more timid kiss,
While the fountain took no share
In the whispers of frenzied love
But pleasure only in its own splashing,
And we could hear the far
Friendly voices,
Flutes and strings,
Taunting and enticing us in vain.

Her dear light head
Lay weary in my arms, too soon
For my desiring. Playfully I pressed
My eyes on hers and felt for a while
Her long eyelashes, until sleep
Stilled them,
Rise and fall like plumes of a butterfly.

Before the sun rose,
Before the lamp in our bridal chamber was quenched,
I woke the sleeper,
Led the strange child into my house.

III

Ein Irrsal kam in die Mondscheingärten
Einer einst heiligen Liebe.
Schaudernd entdeckt' ich verjährten Betrug.
Und mit weinendem Blick, doch grausam,
Hieß ich das schlanke,
Zauberhafte Mädchen
Ferne gehen von mir.
Ach, ihre hohe Stirn
War gesenkt, denn sie liebte mich;
Aber sie zog mit Schweigen
Fort in die graue
Welt hinaus.

Krank seitdem,
Wund ist und wehe mein Herz.
Nimmer wird es genesen!

Als ginge, luftgesponnen, ein Zauberfaden
Von ihr zu mir, ein ängstig Band,
So zieht es, zieht mich schmachtend ihr nach!
—Wie? wenn ich eines Tags auf meiner Schwelle
Sie sitzen fände, wie einst, im Morgen-Zwielicht,
Das Wanderbündel neben ihr,
Und ihr Auge, treuherzig zu mir aufschauend,
Sagte, da bin ich wieder
Hergekommen aus weiter Welt!

IV

Warum, Geliebte, denk ich dein
Auf einmal nun mit tausend Tränen,
Und kann gar nicht zufrieden sein,
Und will die Brust in alle Weite dehnen?

Ach, gestern in den hellen Kindersaal,
Beim Flimmer zierlich aufgesteckter Kerzen,
Wo ich mein selbst vergaß in Lärm und Scherzen,
Tratst du, o Bildnis mitleid-schöner Qual;

III

Into the moonlit gardens of a love once holy,
Wrongness came.
I found with a shudder
She had deceived me long ago.
And with tears, but cruelly,
I told the slender
Magical girl
To go from me.
Ah, her high forehead
Was bowed, for she loved me;
But she went away,
In silence,
Into the gray world.

Since then my heart
Is sick and sore and wounded,
It never will be well again.

As if between herself and me, braided of air,
A magic thread were tied, a timorous bond,
And it draws me, draws me languishing toward her.
—How would it be if one day at my door
I found her sitting as once, in the dusk of sunrise,
Her traveling bundle beside her,
And if her eyes, looking up at me with candor,
Said: Well, here I am,
Back again from the wide wide world!

IV

Suddenly weeping as the thoughts return,
Why do I think of you, my love, like this?
And why with discontent forever burn
And want my heart to fill the world's wide distances?

Ah, into the room of children yesterday,
With candles flickering gracefully and tall,
As I forgot myself in the noise and play,
You came, with pain and pity beautiful;

Es war dein Geist, er setzte sich ans Mahl,
Fremd saßen wir mit stumm verhaltnen Schmerzen;
Zuletzt brach ich in lautes Schluchzen aus,
Und Hand in Hand verließen wir das Haus.

V

Die Liebe, sagt man, steht am Pfahl gebunden,
Geht endlich arm, zerrüttet, unbeschuht;
Dies edle Haupt hat nicht mehr, wo es ruht,
Mit Tränen netzet sie der Füße Wunden.

Ach, Peregrinen habe ich so gefunden!
Schön war ihr Wahnsinn, ihrer Wange Glut,
Noch scherzend in der Frühlingsstürme Wut,
Und wilde Kränze in das Haar gewunden.

War's möglich, solche Schönheit zu verlassen?
—So kehrt nur reizender das alte Glück!
O komm, in diese Arme dich zu fassen!

Doch weh! o weh! was soll mir dieser Blick?
Sie küßt mich zwischen Lieben noch und Hassen,
Sie kehrt sich ab, und kehrt mir nie zurück.

Der Gärtner

Auf ihrem Leibrößlein,
So weiß wie der Schnee,
Die schönste Prinzessin
Reit't durch die Allee.

Der Weg, den das Rößlein
Hintanzet so hold,
Der Sand, den ich streute,
Er blinket wie Gold.

It was your ghost that came to share our meal,
We sat like strangers, grieving the words away,
Until at last I broke out sobbing, and
We left the house together, hand in hand.

V

Love, so they say, is martyred at the stake,
And walks unshod, poor, broken in mind.
No resting place this noble head can find;
Love laves the wounded feet for loving's sake.

Ah, thus I found Peregrina, found her fair
In all her madness, and her way of blushing;
She'd laugh amid the furious storms of spring,
And put wild flower garlands in her hair.

How could I ever forsake such loveliness?
—The joys gone by, more joyous yet, in vain—
Come to my arms, come back to my embrace!

But O, her telling look, and O, the pain!
Loving and hating me she gives her kiss.
She turns away, she'll not come back again.

Christopher Middleton

The Gardener

Upon her pet pony,
    As white as the snow,
The king's fairest daughter
    A-riding doth go.

Down dances her pony
    The avenue old;
Where sand I have scattered
    It sparkles like gold.

Du rosenfarbs Hütlein,
Wohl auf und wohl ab,
O wirf eine Feder
Verstohlen herab!

Und willst du dagegen
Eine Blüte von mir,
Nimm tausend für *eine*,
Nimm alle dafür!

Schön-Rohtraut

Wie heißt König Ringangs Töchterlein?
Rohtraut, Schön-Rohtraut.
Was tut sie denn den ganzen Tag,
Da sie wohl nicht spinnen und nähen mag?
Tut fischen und jagen.
O daß ich doch ihr Jäger wär!
Fischen und Jagen freute mich sehr.
—Schweig stille; mein Herze!

Und über eine kleine Weil,
Rohtraut, Schön-Rohtraut,
So dient der Knab auf Ringangs Schloß
In Jägertracht und hat ein Roß,
Mit Rohtraut zu jagen.
O daß ich doch ein Königssohn wär!
Rohtraut, Schön-Rohtraut lieb ich so sehr.
—Schweig stille, mein Herze!

Einsmals sie ruhten am Eichenbaum,
Da lacht Schön-Rohtraut:
„Was siehst mich an so wunniglich?
Wenn du das Herz hast, küsse mich!"
Ach! erschrak der Knabe!

You rosy-hued bonnet
   There bobbing so high,
O toss me in passing
   A plume on the sly!

And if to my flowers
   Your fancy should range,
For one take a thousand,
   Take all in exchange!

Geoffrey Herbert Chase

Fair Rohtraut

Oh, what is the name of King Ringang's daughter?
Rohtraut, Fair Rohtraut.
And what does she do the live-long day,
Since she scarcely would spin and knit alway?
She goes fishing and hunting.
Oh, that her huntsman I might be!
I'd fish and hunt right merrily.
—Ah, be silent, my heart!

And after just a little while,
Rohtraut, Fair Rohtraut,
The lad did serve at Ringang's court
In squire's garb and had a horse,
To hunt with Rohtraut.
Oh, that a king's son I might be!
I love Fair Rohtraut tenderly.
—Ah, be silent, my heart!

One day they stopped by an old oak tree,
Then laughted Fair Rohtraut:
"Why look at me so blissfully?
If you have courage, come, kiss me!"
Oh, how startled the lad was!

Doch denket er: „Mir ist's vergunnt",
Und küsset Schön-Rohtraut auf den Mund.
—Schweig stille, mein Herze!

Darauf sie ritten schweigend heim,
Rohtraut, Schön-Rohtraut;
Es jauchzt der Knab in seinem Sinn!
„Und würdst du heute Kaiserin,
Mich sollt's nicht kränken!
Ihr tausend Blätter im Walde wißt,
Ich hab Schön-Rohtrauts Mund geküßt!
—Schweig stille, mein Herze!"

Auf eine Lampe

Noch unverrückt, o schöne Lampe, schmückest du,
An leichten Ketten zierlich aufgehangen hier,
Die Decke des nun fast vergeßnen Lustgemachs.
Auf deiner weißen Marmorschale, deren Rand
Der Efeukranz von goldengrünem Erz umflicht,
Schlingt fröhlich eine Kinderschar den Ringelreihn.
Wie reizend alles! lachend, und ein sanfter Geist
Des Ernstes doch ergossen um die ganze Form—
Ein Kunstgebild der echten Art. Wer achtet sein?
Was aber schön ist, selig scheint es in ihm selbst.

Um Mitternacht

Gelassen stieg die Nacht ans Land,
Lehnt träumend an der Berge Wand,
Ihr Auge sieht die goldne Waage nun
Der Zeit in gleichen Schalen stille ruhn;
   Und kecker rauschen die Quellen hervor,

And yet he thinks: " 'Twas offered me,"
And kisses Fair Rohtraut tenderly.
—Ah, be silent, my heart!

And then they rode quite silent home,
Rohtraut, Fair Rohtraut;
The lad exulted all the way:
Though you were made an Empress today,
It would not grieve me;
Ye thousand leaves in the forest, hear!
I've kissed Fair Rohtraut's mouth so dear!
Ah, be silent, my heart!

Isabel S. MacInnes

On a Lamp

Still here in place, o lovely lamp, you decorate,
Having been hung so gracefully from lightweight chains,
The ceiling of the half-forgotten pleasance room.
Upon your marble bowl of white, along whose edge
Ivy is braided in a wreath of gold-green bronze,
A round dance, children winding in a happy band.
It's all so charming! laughing, and a gentle spirit
Of seriousness is poured, still, over the whole form—
A work of art, the genuine kind. Who cares for it?
What's lovely, though, looks radiant from a bliss within.

Joseph B. Dallett

At Midnight

Serene, her landing; dreaming still,
Night leans against the wall of hills;
She watches now time's golden balance cease
From tilting, views the poise of scales at peace.
    And gushing fresher, the springs flow along,

Sie singen der Mutter, der Nacht, ins Ohr
  Vom Tage,
Vom heute gewesenen Tage.

Das uralt alte Schlummerlied,
Sie achtets nicht, sie ist es müd;
Ihr klingt des Himmels Bläue süßer noch,
Der flüchtgen Stunden gleichgeschwungnes Joch.
  Doch immer behalten die Quellen das Wort,
  Es singen die Wasser im Schlafe noch fort
    Vom Tage,
  Vom heute gewesenen Tage.

Nimmersatte Liebe

So ist die Lieb! So ist die Lieb!
Mit Küssen nicht zu stillen:
Wer ist der Tor und will ein Sieb
Mit eitel Wasser füllen?
Und schöpfst du an die tausend Jahr,
Und küssest ewig, ewig gar,
Du tust ihr nie zu Willen.

Die Lieb, die Lieb hat alle Stund
Neu wunderlich Gelüsten;
Wir bissen uns die Lippen wund,
Da wir uns heute küßten.
Das Mädchen hielt in guter Ruh,
Wie's Lämmlein unterm Messer;
Ihr Auge bat: nur immer zu,
Je weher, desto besser!

So ist die Lieb, und war auch so,
Wie lang es Liebe gibt,
Und anders war Herr Salomo,
Der Weise, nicht verliebt.

They sing for the Mother, for Night, their song
   Of the day,
   Of the day that has been today.

So old, this slumber-song of yore,
She's tired of it, she heeds no more;
To her, a sweeter ring's the blue of sky,
Their yoke swung level as the Hours fleet by,
  But always the word is borne on by the springs,
  And while it is sleeping the water still sings
   Of the day,
   Of the day that has been today.

Joseph B. Dallett

Never-sated Love

Such, such is love! Yes, such is love!
With kisses none can still it.
Who is the fool that has a sieve,
And would with water fill it?
A thousand years though were your task
To kiss till love for mercy ask,
You never could fulfil it.

Love's appetite with each new hour
Keeps wondrously increasing;
When long and close we kissed today,
Our lips were sore with kissing.
The maiden suffered like a lamb
The kisses that beset her,
And still her eyes besought: "Keep on!
The more it hurts, the better!"

Love was and ever shall be so,
As long as love endure;
Not otherwise loved Solomon,
That sage old epicure.

Geoffrey Herbert Chase

Zitronenfalter im April

Grausame Frühlingssonne,
Du weckst mich vor der Zeit,
Dem nur in Maienwonne
Die zarte Kost gedeiht!
Ist nicht ein liebes Mädchen hier,
Das auf der Rosenlippe mir
Ein Tröpfchen Honig beut,
So muß ich jämmerlich vergehn
Und wird der Mai mich nimmer sehn
In meinem gelben Kleid.

Erstes Liebeslied eines Mädchens

Was im Netze? Schau einmal!
Aber ich bin bange;
Greif' ich einen süßen Aal?
Greif' ich eine Schlange?

Lieb' ist blinde
Fischerin;
Sagt dem Kinde,
Wo greift's hin?

Schon schnellt mir's in Händen!
Ach Jammer! o Lust!
Mit Schmiegen und Wenden
Mir schlüpft's an die Brust.

Es beißt sich, o Wunder!
Mir keck durch die Haut,
Schießt's Herze hinunter!
O Liebe, mir graut!

Brimstone Butterfly in April

O cruel April sunshine,
Too soon you wake me up;
I thrive but on the dainties
Of May's enchanting cup.
And if no maiden sweet there be,
Whose rosy lips will offer me
A sip of honey dew,
Then wretched, must I surely die,
And May will never see me fly,
Dressed in my yellow hue.

Geoffrey Herbert Chase

Girl's First Love Song

Look, in the net
What's this? I feel
Afraid, am I touching
A snake or an eel?

Love's a fishergirl,
Blind, blind,
Say where it's going,
Comfort her mind.

It whips through my hands,
What pleasures, they hurt!
Coiling and snuggling
Inside my shirt!

Bites clean through my skin,
Now what's this, and O
It shoots my heart down
And frightens me so.

Was tun, was beginnen?
Das schaurige Ding,
Es schnalzet da drinnen,
Es legt sich im Ring.

Gift muß ich haben!
Hier schleicht es herum,
Tut wonniglich graben
Und bringt mich noch um!

Das verlassene Mägdlein

Früh, wann die Hähne krähn,
Eh' die Sternlein verschwinden,
Muß ich am Herde stehn,
Muß Feuer zünden.

Schön ist der Flamme Schein,
Es springen die Funken;
Ich schaue so drein,
In Leid versunken.

Plötzlich, da kommt es mir,
Treuloser Knabe,
Daß ich die Nacht von dir
Geträumet habe.

Träne auf Träne dann
Stürzet hernieder;
So kommt der Tag heran—
O ging er wieder!

Help! What can I do?
The horrible thing,
Smacking its lips,
It coils in a ring.

Its poison has got me,
The cunning, the sly,
The sweet burrowing creature,
I'm certain to die.

Christopher Middleton

The Forsaken Girl

Early, in starlight still,
And the cocks crowing,
I must stand at the hob,
Must get the fire going.

Sparks leap, and lovely
The flames ablaze;
Sunk in sorrow,
At them I gaze.

Suddenly then recall,
Faithless lover,
Last night I dreamed of you,
Over and over.

Tear upon tear now
Tumbling down;
So the day comes and comes—
Would it were gone.

Christopher Middleton

Im Park

Sieh, der Kastanie kindliches Laub hängt noch wie der feuchte
  Flügel des Papillons, wenn er die Hülle verließ;
Aber in laulicher Nacht der kürzeste Regen entfaltet
  Leise die Fächer und deckt schnelle den luftigen Gang.
—Du magst eilen, o himmlischer Frühling, oder verweilen,
  Immer dem trunkenen Sinn fliehst du, ein Wunder, vorbei.

Die schöne Buche

Ganz verborgen im Wald kenn ich ein Plätzchen, da stehet
  Eine Buche, man sieht schöner im Bilde sie nicht.
Rein und glatt, in gediegenem Wuchs erhebt sie sich einzeln,
  Keiner der Nachbarn rührt ihr an den seidenen Schmuck.
Rings, soweit sein Gezweig der stattliche Baum ausbreitet,
  Grünet der Rasen, das Aug still zu erquicken, umher;
Gleich nach allen Seiten umzirkt er den Stamm in der Mitte;
  Kunstlos schuf die Natur selber dies liebliche Rund.
Zartes Gebüsch umkränzet es erst; hochstämmige Bäume,
  Folgend in dichtem Gedräng, wehren dem himmlischen Blau.
Neben der dunkleren Fülle des Eichbaums wiegt die Birke
  Ihr jungfräuliches Haupt schüchtern im goldenen Licht.
Nur wo, verdeckt vom Felsen, der Fußsteig jäh sich hinabschlingt,
  Lässet die Hellung mich ahnen das offene Feld.
—Als ich unlängst einsam, von neuen Gestalten des Sommers
  Ab dem Pfade gelockt, dort im Gebüsch mich verlor,
Führt' ein freundlicher Geist, des Hains auflauschende Gottheit,
  Hier mich zum erstenmal, plötzlich, den Staunenden, ein.
Welch Entzücken! Es war um die hohe Stunde des Mittags,
  Lautlos alles, es schwieg selber der Vogel im Laub.
Und ich zauderte noch, auf den zierlichen Teppich zu treten;
  Festlich empfing er den Fuß, leise beschritt ich ihn nur.

In the Park

Look how the chestnut's childlike foliage hangs like the moistened
  Wing of the butterfly when it has left the cocoon;
But in the temperate night the briefest rain opens gently
  Fan after fan and roofs quickly the airy allee.
—Whether you hurry, o heavenly spring, or linger, you always
  Seem as you fleet past drunk senses the marvel you are!

Joseph B. Dallett

The Lovely Beech

Hidden deep in the woods I know a place where a beech-tree
  Stands—there could never be seen pictured a lovelier one—,
Rising all by itself in its massive development, clean and
  Smooth; of its neighbors none touches its silken attire.
Ringing it, just as far as the stately tree spreads its branches,
  Green turf stretches about, quietly fresh'ning the eye;
Circles, on all sides equidistant, the trunk in the middle.
  Artlessly, Nature herself fashioned this round in its charm.
Wreathing it first are tender shrubs, succeeded by lofty
  Trunks of a thick press of trees, barring the heavenly blue.
Next to the darkish clump of the oak, with shyness the birch-tree
  Sways her virginal head up in the gold of the light.
Only the bright'ning from where the footpath, concealed by the
    rock, twists
  Steeply down can for me hint at the open, the field.
—Not long ago when, quite alone, I was coaxed by the summer's
  New shapes off from the trail, losing myself in the shrubs,
It was a friendly spirit, the listening grove-god, that led me
  In for the very first time here, to my sudden surprise.
What entrancement! The hour was high noon: silence in all things,
  Midday brought to a hush even the bird in the leaves.
Holding back still from walking upon the delicate carpet,
  Ever so softly I set foot on its springy delight.

Jetzo gelehnt an den Stamm (er trägt sein breites Gewölbe
   Nicht zu hoch), ließ ich rundum die Augen ergehn,
Wo den beschatteten Kreis die feurig strahlende Sonne,
   Fast gleich messend umher, säumte mit blendendem Rand.
Aber ich stand und rührte mich nicht; dämonischer Stille,
   Unergründlicher Ruh lauschte mein innerer Sinn.
Eingeschlossen mit dir in diesem sonnigen Zauber-
   Gürtel, o Einsamkeit, fühlt ich und dachte nur dich!

Göttliche Reminiszenz

πάντα δι' αὐτοῦ ἐγένετο
Ev. John. I, 3

Vorlängst sah ich ein wundersames Bild gemalt,
Im Kloster der Kartäuser, das ich oft besucht.
Heut, da ich im Gebirge droben einsam ging,
Umstarrt von wild zerstreuter Felsentrümmersaat,
Trat es mit frischen Farben vor die Seele mir.
An jäher Steinkluft, deren dünn begraster Saum,
Von zweien Palmen überschattet, magre Kost
Den Ziegen beut, den steilauf weidenden am Hang,
Sieht man den Knaben Jesus sitzend auf Gestein;
Ein weißes Vließ als Polster ist ihm unterlegt.
Nicht allzu kindlich deuchte mir das schöne Kind;
Der heiße Sommer, sicherlich sein fünfter schon,
Hat seine Glieder, welche bis zum Knie herab
Das gelbe Röckchen decket mit dem Purpursaum,
Hat die gesunden, zarten Wangen sanft gebräunt;
Aus schwarzen Augen leuchtet stille Feuerkraft,
Den Mund jedoch umfremdet unnennbarer Reiz.
Ein alter Hirte, freundlich zu dem Kind gebeugt,
Gab ihm soeben ein versteinert Meergewächs,
Seltsam gestaltet, in die Hand zum Zeitvertreib.
Der Knabe hat das Wunderding beschaut, und jetzt,
Gleichsam betroffen, spannet sich der weite Blick,

Now I leaned on the trunk (it carries its spreading vault at
  None too great a height), sending my eyes all around,
Where along the rim of the shadowy circle the dazzling
  Sunbeams blazed in an arch just about perfectly drawn.
I stood motionless meanwhile, listened inwardly, sensing
  Strangely compelling calm, peace altogether profound.
Being enclosed with you in this sunny magical cincture,
  Solitude, I felt you, thought you and nothing but you.

Joseph B. Dallett

Divine Reminiscence

All things were made by him
    John 1:3

I saw a marvel of a picture long ago
In the Carthusian cloister where I used to stay.
Today, up in the mountains on a lonely walk—
Stony debris strewn wildly on all sides like seed—
It came to me, in vivid colors, once again.
Beside a steep ravine, whose edge of patchy grass,
Shaded by two palm trees, provides the goats that graze
Uphill along the slope with meagre fare, one sees
The young boy Jesus sitting on the rock; a white
Fleece has been laid down for a cushion under him.
The lovely child, I thought, is not all that childlike;
From the hot summer, certainly his fifth by now,
His healthy, tender cheeks are lightly tanned, his limbs
As well (a little yellow skirt goes to the knee,
The hem is purple); and there gleams from his dark eyes
A quiet fiery power; his mouth, though, has a grace
Setting it off that's strangely indefinable.
An aged shepherd, bending down in friendliness,
Has placed in the child's hand a fossil from the sea,
Quite curious in shape, to while away the time.
This wondrous thing the boy has looked at; now, as if
Bemused, his distant gaze spans out towards you, yet

Entgegen dir, doch wirklich ohne Gegenstand,
Durchdringend ewge Zeiten-Fernen, grenzenlos:
Als wittre durch die überwölkte Stirn ein Blitz
Der Gottheit, ein Erinnern, das im gleichen Nu
Erloschen sein wird; und das welterschaffende,
Das Wort von Anfang, als ein spielend Erdenkind
Mit Lächeln zeigts unwissend dir sein eigen Werk.

Auf eine Christblume

I

Tochter des Walds, du Lilienverwandte,
So lang von mir gesuchte, unbekannte,
Im fremden Kirchhof, öd und winterlich,
Zum erstenmal, o schöne, find ich dich!

Von welcher Hand gepflegt du hier erblühtest,
Ich weiß es nicht, noch wessen Grab du hütest;
Ist es ein Jüngling, so geschah ihm Heil,
Ists eine Jungfrau, lieblich fiel ihr Teil.

Im nächtgen Hain, von Schneelicht überbreitet,
Wo fromm das Reh an dir vorüberweidet,
Bei der Kapelle, am kristallnen Teich,
Dort sucht ich deiner Heimat Zauberreich.

Schön bist du, Kind des Mondes, nicht der Sonne;
Dir wäre tödlich andrer Blumen Wonne,
Dich nährt, den keuschen Leib voll Reif und Duft,
Himmlischer Kälte balsamsüße Luft.

It really has no object; penetrating through
Remotest time's eternal stretches, boundlessly,
As if the lightning of divinity, recalled,
Is shooting through the clouded forehead, but will go
Out in this selfsame instant; and the primal Word
Making the world, it shows you, as an earthly child
Smiling at play, unknowingly its work, its own.

Joseph B. Dallett

On a Christmas Rose

I

In this bare, wintry, unfamiliar burying-ground,
O daughter of the woods, akin
to lilies, sought so long, unknown before, I've found
you, lovely one!
My search is done.

I can but wonder through whose caring hand you flowered
here; whose grave it is you guard;
if it's a girl—gracious the way that she was dowered;
if it's a boy—
blessed in joy.

I would explore
the land that bore
you—realm of magic—in the grove decked with snowlight,
where docile roe goes grazing by you in the night,
at the chapel and the crystal pond.

O lovely moon-child, you're not of the sun, and dead
you'd be from other flowers' bliss;
cold heaven's sweet nutrient air's the balm with which you're fed—
chaste body's fill
of frost-scent's chill.

In deines Busens goldner Fülle gründet
Ein Wohlgeruch, der sich nur kaum verkündet;
So duftete, berührt von Engelshand,
Der benedeiten Mutter Brautgewand.

Dich würden, mahnend an das heilge Leiden,
Fünf Purpurtropfen schön und einzig kleiden:
Doch kindlich zierst du, um die Weihnachtszeit,
Lichtgrün mit einem Hauch dein weißes Kleid.

Der Elfe, der in mitternächtger Stunde
Zum Tanze geht im lichterhellen Grunde,
Vor deiner mystischen Glorie steht er scheu
Neugierig still von fern und huscht vorbei.

II

Im Winterboden schläft, ein Blumenkeim,
Der Schmetterling, der einst um Busch und Hügel
In Frühlingsnächten wiegt den sanften Flügel;
Nie soll er kosten deinen Honigseim.

Wer aber weiß, ob nicht sein zarter Geist,
Wenn jede Zier des Sommers hingesunken,
Dereinst, von deinem leisen Dufte trunken,
Mir unsichtbar, dich blühende umkreist?

Merest annunciation is the fragrance down
within your bosom's golden room;
so also with the Blessed Mother's bridal gown;
its scent was such
at angel's touch.

Lovely in fivefold purple drops you would suggest
the sacred Passion by yourself;
and yet at Christmas time how like a child you're dressed:
a breath of light-
green on your white.

The elf, who's out
to dance about
at midnight in the glowing hollow, he is shy
before your mystic glory, stands
far off, immobile, curious, and flits on by.

II

Waiting in winter sleep to flower from underground,
the butterfly will hover over bush and mound
with silken wing
at night, come spring—
never to taste your honied sweets.

Perhaps, though, after summer's whole embellishment
subsides, its tender ghost, drunk with your fragile scent,
will come, though I
cannot descry
it, circling round you blossoming.

Joseph B. Dallett

Septembermorgen

Im Nebel ruhet noch die Welt,
Noch träumen Wald und Wiesen:
Bald siehst du, wenn der Schleier fällt,
Den blauen Himmel unverstellt,
Herbstkräftig die gedämpfte Welt
In warmem Golde fließen.

Friedrich Hebbel

Sommerbild

Ich sah des Sommers letzte Rose stehn,
Sie war, als ob sie bluten könne, rot;
Da sprach ich schauernd im Vorübergehn:
"So weit im Leben ist zu nah am Tod!"

Es regte sich kein Hauch am heißen Tag,
Nur leise strich ein weißer Schmetterling;
Doch, ob auch kaum die Luft sein Flügelschlag
Bewegte, sie empfand es und verging.

September Morning

   Sleeps the world still
In folds of mist.
   Meadow and woodland
Still are dreaming.
   Soon when the veil
Down has slid,
   You shall see
Blue sky manifest
   And autumn-vivid
The calm world amid
   A warm gold streaming.

       Christopher Middleton

Friedrich Hebbel

Summer Scene

'Twas the last rose of summer that I saw,
so red, it seemed to me, the bloom could bleed;
I thought in passing, senses filled with awe,
death lies so near life's ripe maturity.

No movement marred the stillness of that hour,
save the white fluttering of a butterfly;
but though its gentle rhythm hardly stirred
the air, the rose was touched, and had to die.

       Thomas Kerth

Herbstbild

Dies ist ein Herbsttag, wie ich keinen sah!
Die Luft ist still, als atmete man kaum,
Und dennoch fallen raschelnd, fern und nah,
Die schönsten Früchte ab von jedem Baum.

O stört sie nicht, die Feier der Natur!
Dies ist die Lese, die sie selber hält,
Denn heute löst sich von den Zweigen nur,
Was vor dem milden Strahl der Sonne fällt.

Der Baum in der Wüste

Es steht ein Baum im Wüstensand,
Der einzige, der dort gedieh;
Die Sonne hat ihn fast verbrannt,
Der Regen tränkt den durst'gen nie.

In seiner falben Krone hängt
Gewürzig eine Frucht voll Saft,
Er hat sein Mark hineingedrängt,
Sein Leben, seine höchste Kraft.

Die Stunde, wo sie, überschwer,
Zu Boden fallen muß, ist nah,
Es zieht kein Wanderer daher,
Und für ihn selbst ist sie nicht da.

Image of Autumn

This is an autumn day beyond compare!
The world scarce seems to breathe, the air's so still,
And yet from every tree, now here, now there,
The choicest fruits with gentle rustling spill.

Let none disturb the feast by nature held!
This is the harvest that she calls her own,
For on this day from every branch is culled
What falls before the sun's mild rays alone.

Gerd Gillhoff

The Tree in the Desert

In the sanded desert stands a tree,
    Alive, alone in a land accurst.
The sun has burnt him cruelly;
    No dew or raindrop cools his thirst.

His withered leaves are brightened with
    A single fruit. Her spicy skin
Swells tight with sap and all the pith
    Of life and force the tree pressed in.

The heavy hour nears when she
    Must fall and leave his branches bare.
There comes no wanderer to the tree
    And for himself she is not there.

Herman and Marion Salinger

Sie sehn sich nicht wieder

Von dunkelnden Wogen
Hinuntergezogen,
Zwei schimmernde Schwäne, sie schiffen daher.
Die Winde, sie schwellen
Allmählich die Wellen,
Die Nebel, sie senken sich finster und schwer.

Die Schwäne, sie meiden
Einander und leiden,
Nun tun sie es nicht mehr, sie können die Glut
Nicht länger verschließen,
Sie wollen genießen,
Verhüllt von den Nebeln, gewiegt von der Flut.

Sie schmeicheln, sie kosen,
Sie trotzen dem Tosen
Der Wellen, die Zweie in Eines verschränkt,
Wie die sich auch bäumen,
Sie glühen und träumen,
In Liebe und Wonne zum Sterben versenkt.

Nach innigem Gatten
Ein süßes Ermatten,
Da trennt sie die Woge, bevor sie's gedacht.
Laßt ruhn das Gefieder!
Ihr seht euch nicht wieder,
Der Tag ist vorüber, es dämmert die Nacht.

They Will Meet No More

Drawn by the dark current,
Swept downward, swept errant,
Two swans shimmer white, and their course is away.
The winds, waxing stronger,
Lift surfs ever longer,
The mists gather heavy to end the light's sway.

They shun one another,
The swans, though they suffer,
Yet now cease their shunning, and cannot restrain
The flames that enfold them,
And let pleasure hold them,
Concealed by the fogbanks, rocked by the waves' train.

Their play, their cajoling
Defy the wild rolling
That buffets the two of them, woven to one,
Despite the waves' streaming
They burn in their dreaming,
And are to their rapture, a very death, come.

Then after love's joined them,
Sweet sloth falls upon them,
And swift the tide parts them, before they're aware.
Your wings—let them rest now!
You will meet no more now,
The daytime is past, and night darkens the air.

G. C. Schoolfield

Theodor Storm

Die Stadt

Am grauen Strand, am grauen Meer
Und seitab liegt die Stadt;
Der Nebel drückt die Dächer schwer,
Und durch die Stille braust das Meer
Eintönig um die Stadt.

Es rauscht kein Wald, es schlägt im Mai
Kein Vogel ohn' Unterlaß;
Die Wandergans mit hartem Schrei
Nur fliegt in Herbstesnacht vorbei,
Am Strande weht das Gras.

Doch hängt mein ganzes Herz an dir,
Du graue Stadt am Meer;
Der Jugend Zauber für und für
Ruht lächelnd doch auf dir, auf dir,
Du graue Stadt am Meer.

Meeresstrand

Ans Haff nun fliegt die Möwe,
Und Dämmrung bricht herein;
Über die feuchten Watten
Spiegelt der Abendschein.

Graues Geflügel huschet
Neben dem Wasser her;
Wie Träume liegen die Inseln
Im Nebel auf dem Meer.

Theodor Storm

The Town

Grey is the shore, grey is the sea
And near it stands the town;
The fogs weigh down the old roof-trees
And through the silence roars the sea
Unceasing round the town.

There are no rustling woods, there fly
No singing birds in May;
The wild goose with its grating cry
In autumn nights alone wings by,
The shoreline grasses sway.

And yet my whole heart hangs on you,
Grey town beside the sea;
The spell of youth rests through and through,
Rests smiling still on you, on you,
Grey town beside the sea.

R. M. Browning

The Seashore

Laguneward flies the seagull
As day gives way to night.
The wet-glazed flats at ebbtide
Reflect the evening light.

Gray fowl in flocks are darting
Close to the water's brim.
Like dreams appear the islands
In mist, remote and dim.

Ich höre des gärenden Schlammes
Geheimnisvollen Ton,
Einsames Vogelrufen—
So war es immer schon.

Noch einmal schauert leise
Und schweiget dann der Wind;
Vernehmlich werden die Stimmen,
Die über der Tiefe sind.

Über die Heide

Über die Heide hallet mein Schritt;
Dumpf aus der Erde wandert es mit.

Herbst ist gekommen, Frühling ist weit—
Gab es denn einmal selige Zeit?

Brauende Nebel geisten umher;
Schwarz ist das Kraut, und der Himmel so leer.

Wär' ich hier nur nicht gegangen im Mai!
Leben und Liebe,—wie flog es vorbei!

Hyazinthen

Fern hallt Musik; doch hier ist stille Nacht,
Mit Schlummerduft anhauchen mich die Pflanzen:
Ich habe immer, immer dein gedacht;
Ich möchte schlafen, aber du mußt tanzen.

Es hört nicht auf, es rast ohn' Unterlaß;
Die Kerzen brennen, und die Geigen schreien,

I hear the eerie ferment
In mud banks off the shore,
The lonely cries of the seabirds—
Thus was it evermore.

Again the wind wails softly,
Then slowly sinks to sleep,
And now are heard the voices
That hover over the deep.

Gerd Gillhoff

Over the Moorland

Over the moorland my hollow steps go:
hollow they echo up from below.

Autumn is come, spring and summer gone by—
Say: was there ever a season of joy?

Swirling mists now haunt the heath,
the skies are black as the grass beneath.

Oh had I only not walked here in May!
Loving and living how fast fled away!

Herman Salinger

Hyacinths

Far music rings; here night is still and blue,
Full of the slumbrous perfume of the plants.
My thoughts have only, only been of you;
I long to sleep, but you must dance and dance.

It rages on, it does not cease nor fail;
The candles glisten and the viols shrill;

246 · German Poetry from 1750–1900

Es teilen und es schließen sich die Reihen,
Und alle glühen; aber du bist blaß.

Und du mußt tanzen; fremde Arme schmiegen
Sich an dein Herz; o leide nicht Gewalt!
Ich seh dein weißes Kleid vorüberfliegen
Und deine leichte, zärtliche Gestalt.——

Und süßer strömend quillt der Duft der Nacht
Und träumerischer aus dem Kelch der Pflanzen.
Ich habe immer, immer dein gedacht;
Ich möchte schlafen, aber du mußt tanzen.

April

Das ist die Drossel, die da schlägt,
Der Frühling, der mein Herz bewegt;
Ich fühle, die sich hold bezeigen,
Die Geister aus der Erde steigen.
Das Leben fließet wie ein Traum—
Mir ist wie Blume, Blatt und Baum.

Juli

Klingt im Wind ein Wiegenlied,
Sonne warm herniedersieht,
Seine Ähren senkt das Korn,
Rote Beere schwillt am Dorn,
Schwer von Segen ist die Flur—
Junge Frau, was sinnst du nur?

They part and close again in the quadrille,
And all are glowing, only you are pale.

And you must dance; and others' arms are lying
Close to your heart.—O do not suffer harm!
I see your white and gauzy gown go flying
And see your light and delicate young form.—

And sweeter night's sweet essence filters through
And still more dreamy from the dreaming plants.
My thoughts have only, only been of you;
I long to sleep, but you must dance and dance.

Herman Salinger

April

That is the thrush that's singing there,
The Spring that moves my heart to care;
I feel a sweet, propitious striving:
The spirits from the earth are rising.
Dream-like all life is flowing now—
I am part of bloom and blade and bough.

R. M. Browning

July

Sounds in wind a lullaby,
sun shines warmly from the sky,
heavy ears bend down the corn,
berries ripen on the thorn,
fields with richest blessings teem—
young woman, tell me what you dream.

J. W. Thomas

Regine

Und webte noch auf jenen Matten
Noch jene Mondesmärchenpracht,
Und stünd' sie noch im Waldesschatten
Inmitten jener Sommernacht;
Und fänd' ich selber wie im Traume
Den Weg zurück durch Moor und Feld,
Sie schritte doch vom Waldessaume
Niemals hinunter in die Welt.

Schlaflos

Aus Träumen in Ängsten bin ich erwacht;
Was singt doch die Lerche so tief in der Nacht!

Der Tag ist gegangen, der Morgen ist fern,
Aufs Kissen hernieder scheinen die Stern'.

Und immer hör' ich den Lerchengesang;
O Stimme des Tages, mein Herz ist bang.

Gottfried Keller

Abendlied

Augen, meine lieben Fensterlein,
Gebt mir schon so lange holden Schein,
Lasset freundlich Bild um Bild herein
Einmal werdet ihr verdunkelt sein!

Regine

And even if on yonder meadows
Still gleamed that magic lunar light,
And she still stood in forest shadows
Within that selfsame summer night,
And if I found through moor and hedges
My way back there as in a dream,
She'd never from the woodland's edges
Step back into the world again.

John E. Rothensteiner, rev. by
R. M. Browning

Sleepless

From dreams of foreboding I waken in fright;
Why is the lark singing so deep in the night?

Day has departed, morning is far,
Here on my pillow, light of a star.

And still I hear it, the lark's song clear;
O voice of midday, my heart's full of fear.

R. M. Browning

Gottfried Keller

Evening Song

Eyes, my windows, eyes my fond delight,
Giving me a life-time's cherished light,
Letting pictures in, so kind, so right,
Darkness lies in wait for you, and night.

Fallen einst die müden Lider zu,
Löscht ihr aus, dann hat die Seele Ruh;
Tastend streift sie ab die Wanderschuh,
Legt sich auch in ihre finstre Truh.

Noch zwei Fünklein sieht sie glimmend stehn
Wie zwei Sternlein, innerlich zu sehn,
Bis sie schwanken und dann auch vergehn,
Wie von eines Falters Flügelwehn.

Doch noch wandl' ich auf dem Abendfeld,
Nur dem sinkenden Gestirn gesellt;
Trinkt, o Augen, was die Wimper hält,
Von dem goldnen Überfluß der Welt!

Siehst du den Stern

Siehst du den Stern im fernsten Blau,
Der flimmernd fast erbleicht?
Sein Licht braucht eine Ewigkeit,
Bis es dein Aug erreicht!

Vielleicht vor tausend Jahren schon
Zu Asche stob der Stern;
Und doch steht dort sein milder Schein
Noch immer still und fern.

Dem Wesen solchen Scheines gleicht,
Der ist und doch nicht ist,
O Lieb, dein anmutvolles Sein,
Wenn du gestorben bist!

Once the tired lids shut the soul finds peace.
Light extinguished halts her in her race;
Fumbling she will her walking-shoes unlace,
Lie down in a dark and narrow place.

Not utter darkness yet; two embers glow,
Two mind's-eye stars, a prick of light or so;
Flicker, dwindle, waver, then as though
A moth's wing brushed them—puff—and out they go.

Only sun and I afield, untold,
Slanting, late, low beams the world enfold;
Drink, my eyes, drink all your lashes hold
Of the world's flooding, overflowing gold.

K. W. Maurer

See there the star

See there the star. In distant blue
Its twinkle almost dies.
Its light took an eternity
Until it reached your eyes.

A thousand years ago perhaps
In ashes fell that star,
And yet, up there its gentle light
Keeps shining still and far.

Quite like that star, quite like its light
Which shines because it shone,
O love, I sense thy cherished warmth
Since thou art dead and gone.

Alexander Gode

In der Stadt

I

Wo sich drei Gassen kreuzen, krumm und enge,
Drei Züge wallen plötzlich sich entgegen
Und schlingen sich, gehemmt auf ihren Wegen,
Zu einem Knäul und lärmendem Gedränge.

Die Wachtparad mit gellen Trommelschlägen,
Ein Brautzug kommt mit Geigen und Gepränge,
Ein Leichenzug klagt seine Grabgesänge:
Das alles stockt, es kann kein Glied sich regen.

Verstummt sind Geiger, Pfaff und Trommelschläger;
Der dicke Hauptmann flucht, daß niemand weiche,
Gelächter schallet aus dem Freudenzug.

Doch oben, auf den Schultern schwarzer Träger
Starrt in der Mitte kalt und still die Leiche
Mit blinden Augen in den Wolkenflug.

Winternacht

Nicht ein Flügelschlag ging durch die Welt,
Still und blendend lag der weiße Schnee.
Nicht ein Wölklein hing am Sternenzelt,
Keine Welle schlug im starren See.

Aus der Tiefe stieg der Seebaum auf,
Bis sein Wipfel in dem Eis gefror;
An den Ästen klomm die Nix' herauf,
Schaute durch das grüne Eis empor.

Auf dem dünnen Glase stand ich da,
Das die schwarze Tiefe von mir schied;

In the City

I

Where intersect three narrow, crooked lanes,
Three separate groups emerge and headlong meet.
Unable to move forward or retreat,
They lock as in a mass of tangled skeins.

The watch, parading to the drums' shrill beat,
A wedding gay, with fiddlers in its train,
A group of mourners, singing funeral strains,
Slow down perforce till stock-still rest all feet.

Now fiddlers, priest, and drummers silent fall,
The thickset captain rudely curses all,
The members of the party laugh aloud.

But in their midst the black-garbed bearers hold
Aloft the corpse, which, motionless and cold,
Stares up, unseeing, at a drifting cloud.

Gerd Gillhoff

Winter Night

World without a wingbeat in the air,
Silent snow so white one saw no more,
Sky of stars and no cloud anywhere,
Frozen lake where no wave beat the shore.

From the depths the sea-tree grew upright
'Til its crown met ice and in it froze.
On the branches climbed the water-sprite,
Looking through the green ice as she rose.

There I stood, the thin ice under me
Marking off the black abyss below.

Dicht ich unter meinen Füßen sah
Ihre weiße Schönheit, Glied um Glied.

Mit ersticktem Jammer tastet sie
An der harten Decke her und hin,
Ich vergess' das dunkle Antlitz nie;
Immer, immer liegt es mir im Sinn.

Theodor Fontane

Die Brücke am Tay

> 28. *Dezember 1879*
> *When shall we three meet again?* (Macbeth)

„Wann treffen wir drei wieder zusamm?"
„Um die siebente Stund, am Brückendamm."
„Am Mittelpfeiler."
                    „Ich lösche die Flamm."
„Ich mit."
          „Ich komme vom Norden her."
„Und ich vom Süden."
                    „Und ich vom Meer."
„Hei, das gibt einen Ringelreihn,
Und die Brücke muß in den Grund hinein."
„Und der Zug, der in die Brücke tritt
Um die siebente Stund?"
                    „Ei, der muß mit."
„Muß mit."
          „Tand, Tand
Ist das Gebilde von Menschenhand!"

Auf der Norderseite das Brückenhaus—
Alle Fenster sehen nach Süden aus,

Close beneath my feet I still could see
Limb on limb, her beauty white as snow.

Choked with grief she moved from place to place,
Groping underneath the frozen rind.
I can not forget that cold dark face;
It will never, never leave my mind.

Frank G. Ryder

Theodor Fontane

The Bridge on the Tay

December 28, 1879
When shall we three meet again? (Macbeth)

"When shall we three meet again?"
"By the bridge, at seven, down the lane."
"By the middle pier."
                              "I put out the flame."
"I too."
            "I come from the northern sphere."
"And I from the south."
                              "From the sea I come here."
"A merry dance it will be, ho! ho!
And down to the bottom the bridge must go."
"And the train that at seven passes through
To cross the bridge?"
                              "Hey, that goes too."
"Goes too."
            "On sand, on sand,
Rests all that is built by human hand."

The bridgekeeper's house on the bank to the north—
All windows to the south look forth,

Und die Brücknersleut ohne Rast und Ruh
Und in Bangen sehen nach Süden zu,
Sehen und warten, ob nicht ein Licht
Übers Wasser hin „Ich komme "spricht,
„Ich komme, trotz Nacht und Sturmesflug,
Ich, der Edinburger Zug."

Und der Brückner jetzt: „Ich seh einen Schein
Am anderen Ufer. Das muß er sein.
Nun, Mutter, weg mit dem bangen Traum,
Unser Johnie kommt und will seinen Baum,
Und was noch am Baume von Lichtern ist,
Zünd alles an wie zum heiligen Christ,
Der will heuer zweimal mit uns sein—
Und in elf Minuten ist er herein."

Und es war der Zug. Am Süderturm
Keucht er vorbei jetzt gegen den Sturm,
Und Johnie spricht: „Die Brücke noch!
Aber was tut es, wir zwingen es doch.
Ein fester Kessel, ein doppelter Dampf,
Die bleiben Sieger in solchem Kampf.
Und wies auch rast und ringt und rennt,
Wir kriegen es unter, das Element.

Und unser Stolz ist unsre Brück;
Ich lache, denk' ich an früher zurück,
An all den Jammer und all die Not
Mit dem elend alten Schifferboot;
Wie manche liebe Christfestnacht
Hab ich im Fährhaus zugebracht
Und sah unsrer Fenster lichten Schein
Und zählte und konnte nicht drüben sein."

Auf der Norderseite, das Brückenhaus—
Alle Fenster sehen nach Süden aus,
Und die Brücknersleut ohne Rast und Ruh
Und in Bangen sehen nach Süden zu;
Denn wütender wurde der Winde Spiel,

The keeper, his wife, both restlessly peer
Towards the south with growing fear,
They watch and wait for a light to say
"Look out, I am coming" across the bay,
"In spite of the night and the hurricane,
Here I come, the Edinburgh train."

And the bridgekeeper says: "That light shows plain
On the other shore. It must be the train.
Now, mother, have done with your nightmares, you see
Our Johnnie is coming and wants his tree.
What candles are left on the tree, you shall light,
So that all will be as on Christmas Night.
We'll celebrate it twice this year—
In eleven minutes it will be here."

And it was the train. It is panting past
The southern tower and into the blast.
And Johnnie is saying: "The bridge comes yet,
But no matter the challenge, it will be met;
A sturdy boiler and double the steam,
And they will be the winning team.
Though on raging and wrestling and rushing bent,
We'll conquer it yet, the element.

Our bridge that is our biggest boast.
I laugh when I think of the time we lost,
Of all the misery and the cold
In that ferryboat, so wretchedly old;
How many a cherished Christmas Night
I spent in the ferryhouse, within sight
Of our windows, that shone with festive glare,
And counted them, and could not be there."

The bridgekeeper's house on the bank to the north—
All windows to the south look forth,
And the keeper, his wife, both restlessly peer
Towards the south with growing fear;
From playful, the winds had been getting high,

Und jetzt, als ob Feuer vom Himmel fiel,
Erglüht es in niederschießender Pracht
Überm Wasser unten . . . Und wieder ist Nacht.

„Wann treffen wir drei wieder zusamm?"
„Um Mitternacht, am Bergeskamm."
„Auf dem hohen Moor, am Erlenstamm."
„Ich komme."
        „Ich mit."
                 „Ich nenn euch die Zahl."
„Und ich die Namen."
                „Und ich die Qual."
„Hei!
    Wie Splitter brach das Gebälk entzwei."
         „Tand, Tand
Ist das Gebilde von Menschenhand."

Conrad Ferdinand Meyer

Eingelegte Ruder

Meine eingelegten Ruder triefen,
Tropfen fallen langsam in die Tiefen.

Nichts, das mich verdroß! Nichts, das mich freute!
Niederrinnt ein schmerzenloses Heute!

Unter mir—ach, aus dem Licht verschwunden—
Träumen schon die schönern meiner Stunden.

Aus der blauen Tiefe ruft das Gestern:
Sind im Licht noch manche meiner Schwestern?

And now, as though fires poured forth from the sky,
In downshooting splendor all is alight
On the waters below . . . and again it is night.

"When shall we three meet again?"
"At twelve, on the ridge above the plain."
"On the Highland moor, by the alders twain."
"I come."
      "I too."
            "The count I supply."
"And I the names."
            "Their agonies I."
"Hey!
Like sticks the girders broke away!"
            "On sand, on sand,
Rests all that is built by human hand."

Helen Kurz Roberts

Conrad Ferdinand Meyer

With My Oars Pulled Up

Pulled up now my oars are gently dripping,
Drops into the deep are slowly slipping.

Nothing brought me hurt! And nothing gladness!
This today runs down and with no sadness!

Under me—O, hidden from the gleaming
Sunlight—my lovelier hours are dreaming.

From the blue depths yesterday is calling:
Have I sisters yet where light is falling?

John Fitzell

Schwarzschattende Kastanie

Schwarzschattende Kastanie,
Mein windgeregtes Sommerzelt,
Du senkst zur Flut dein weit Geäst,
Dein Laub, es durstet und es trinkt,
Schwarzschattende Kastanie!
Im Porte badet junge Brut
Mit Hader oder Lustgeschrei,
Und Kinder schwimmen leuchtend weiß
Im Gitter deines Blätterwerks,
Schwarzschattende Kastanie!
Und dämmern See und Ufer ein
Und rauscht vorbei das Abendboot,
So zuckt aus roter Schiffslatern
Ein Blitz und wandert auf dem Schwung
Der Flut, gebrochnen Lettern gleich,
Bis unter deinem Laub erlischt
Die rätselhafte Flammenschrift,
Schwarzschattende Kastanie!

Michelangelo und seine Statuen

Du öffnest, Sklave, deinen Mund,
Doch stöhnst du nicht. Die Lippe schweigt.
Nicht drückt, Gedankenvoller, dich
Die Bürde der behelmten Stirn.
Du packst mit nerv'ger Hand den Bart,
Doch springst du, Moses, nicht empor.
Maria mit dem toten Sohn,
Du weinst, doch rinnt die Träne nicht.
Ihr stellt des Leids Gebärde dar,
Ihr meine Kinder, ohne Leid!

Black-shadowing Chestnut Tree

Black-shadowing chestnut tree,
My wind-tossed summer tent,
With spreading limbs you touch the lake,
Your thirsty foliage dips and drinks,
Black-shadowing chestnut tree!
A young brood's bathing in the port
With shouts of strife and shouts of joy,
And children swim there gleaming white
Behind the fretwork of your boughs
Black-shadowing chestnut tree!
When lake and shoreline sink in dusk,
And then the evening boat steams by,
The larboard lantern dartles red
A gleam that wanders with the swell
Like broken letters in the wake,
Until beneath your leaves expires
The undeciphered fiery script,
Black-shadowing chestnut tree!

R. M. Browning

Michelangelo and His Statues

You open wide your mouth, o slave,
But do not groan. Your lip is mute.
The burden of your visored brow
Does not oppress you, pensive one.*
With sinewed hand you grasp your beard,
But spring not, Moses, from your seat.
Maria with the lifeless son,
You weep, but one sees no tear flow.
You show the look of suffering, true,
But you, my children, suffer not!

* *Il pensieroso* (in the funeral monument for the Medici family, San Lorenzo, Florence).

So sieht der freigewordne Geist
Des Lebens überwundne Qual.
Was martert die lebend'ge Brust,
Beseligt und ergötzt im Stein.
Den Augenblick verewigt ihr,
Und sterbt ihr, sterbt ihr ohne Tod.
Im Schilfe wartet Charon mein,
Der pfeifend sich die Zeit vertreibt.

Der römische Brunnen

Aufsteigt der Strahl und fallend gießt
Er voll der Marmorschale Rund,
Die, sich verschleiernd, überfließt
In einer zweiten Schale Grund;
Die zweite gibt, sie wird zu reich,
Der dritten wallend ihre Flut,
Und jede nimmt und gibt zugleich
Und strömt und ruht.

Im Spätboot

Aus der Schiffsbank mach ich meinen Pfühl.
Endlich wird die heiße Stirne kühl!
O wie süß erkaltet mir das Herz!
O wie weich verstummen Lust und Schmerz!
Über mir des Rohres schwarzer Rauch
Wiegt und biegt sich in des Windes Hauch.
Hüben hier und wieder drüben dort
Hält das Boot an manchem kleinen Port:
Bei der Schiffslaterne kargem Schein
Steigt ein Schatten aus und niemand ein.
Nur der Steurer noch, der wacht und steht!

Thus sees the spirit, freedom gained,
Life's torment overcome at last.
What tortures every living breast
Enraptures and delights in stone.
The moment's saved from death by you,
And dying is for you no death.
On shore old Charon waits for me
And whistling whiles the time away.

R. M. Browning

Roman Fountain

Up! Up the jet of water rides
And falling fills the marble round,
Which overspills in veiling tides
That seek the second basin's ground;
Growing too high the second leaves
Its surfeit to the third below
And each one gives and each receives
In rest and flow.

Frank G. Ryder

Last Boat

The ship's bench I make my resting place.
Welcome coolness blows across my face!
O how sweetly now the heart is chilled!
O how gently joy and pain are stilled!
Over me the smoke-stack, black as death,
playing, swaying in the winds' soft breath.
Now this side, now that by arching arbor
our boat stops at many a tiny harbor:
by ship's lantern shine, so faint and dull,
shadows leave the ever emptier hull.
Only still the helmsman watchful stands.

Nur der Wind, der mir im Haare weht!
Schmerz und Lust erleiden sanften Tod.
Einen Schlummrer trägt das dunkle Boot.

Ferdinand von Saar

Auf einen alten Schloßpark

Nie hat die Lust als Ariadnefaden
Sich durch dies grüne Labyrinth gezogen;
Man glättete hier stets des Lebens Wogen
Zum Teich Bethesda, um sich rein zu baden.

Eremitagen, Grotten an den Pfaden
Für schöne Seelen, die sich selbst belogen,
Als sie sich nannten von der Welt betrogen,
Und brünstig sah'n nach himmlischen Gestaden.

Hier stand die Zeit still, die, vom blut'gen Ruhme
Des Korsen kaum befreit, demütig wieder
Zu Füßen sank dem alten Heiligtume.

Hier weh'n noch Matthissons schwermüt'ge Lieder,
Hier blüht und duftet noch die blaue Blume,
Und wandelt Stillings Geist noch auf und nieder.

Only wind blows on my hair and hands.
Pain and joy have lost their heavy grip.
One slumberer still haunts the darkened ship.

Herman Salinger

Ferdinand von Saar

On an Old Castle Park

Desire has never, through this maze's green,
Charted its way like Ariadne's thread;
Here life's waves were always smoothed and led
Into Bethesda's pond, to bathe men clean.

Grottoes and arbors lined this serpentine
For lofty spirits, who each time they said
The world had tricked them, tricked themselves instead,
Dreaming in pious lust of heaven's demesne.

Here time, which from Napoleon's bloody fame
Had scarcely been set free, stood still to pay
Its humble homage at the old god's flame.

Here hang the notes of Matthisson's sad lay,
Here the blue flower's perfume clings the same,
And here the ghost of Stilling goes its way.

G. C. Schoolfield

Friedrich Nietzsche

Ecce homo

Ja! Ich weiss, woher ich stamme!
Ungesättigt gleich der Flamme
glühe und verzehr ich mich.
Licht wird alles, was ich fasse,
Kohle alles, was ich lasse:
Flamme bin ich sicherlich!

Die Sonne sinkt

I

Nicht lange durstest du noch,
    verbranntes Herz!
Verheißung ist in der Luft,
aus unbekannten Mündern bläst michs an,
    —die große Kühle kommt . . .

Meine Sonne stand heiß über mir im Mittage:
seid mir gegrüßt, daß ihr kommt,
    ihr plötzlichen Winde,
ihr kühlen Geister des Nachmittags!

Die Luft geht fremd und rein.
Schielt nicht mit schiefem
    Verführerblick
die Nacht mich an? . . .
Bleib stark, mein tapfres Herz!
Frag nicht: warum?—

Friedrich Nietzsche

Behold the Man!

Yes! I know wherefrom I came!
Ever hungry like a flame
Naught my passion can impede.
All I touch turns first to light,
Then to ashes black as night:
A flame is what I am indeed!

Edward Dvoretzky

The Sun Sinks

I

Not long will you thirst,
  burnt-out heart!
A promise is in the air,
from unknown lips it blows on me
  —the great chill comes.

My sun stood hot over me at noon—
be welcome that you come,
  you sudden winds,
you chilly spirits of afternoon!

The air moves strange and pure.
Does not with warped
  seductive eyes
night leer at me?
Stay strong, courageous heart!
Do not ask: why?

II

Tag meines Lebens!
die Sonne sinkt.
Schon steht die glatte
   Flut vergüldet.
Warm atmet der Fels:
   schlief wohl zu Mittag
das Glück auf ihm seinen Mittagsschlaf?
   In grünen Lichtern
spielt Glück noch der braune Abgrund herauf.

Tag meines Lebens!
gen Abend gehts!
Schon glüht dein Auge
   halbgebrochen,
schon quillt deines Taus
   Tränengeträufel,
schon läuft still über weiße Meere
deiner Liebe Purpur,
deine letzte zögernde Seligkeit . . .

III

Heiterkeit, güldene, komm!
   du des Todes
heimlichster, süßester Vorgenuß!
—Lief ich zu rasch meines Wegs?
Jetzt erst, wo der Fuß müde ward,
   holt dein Blick mich noch ein,
   holt dein *Glück* mich noch ein.

Rings nur Welle und Spiel.
   Was je schwer war,
sank in blaue Vergessenheit,—
müßig steht nun mein Kahn.
Sturm und Fahrt—wie verlernt' er das!
   Wunsch und Hoffen ertrank,
   glatt liegt Seele und Meer.

II

Day of my life!
The sun sinks.
Already the smooth
   flood stands golden.
Warm breathes the rock:
   whether at noon
joy slept its noonday sleep upon it?
   In greenish lights
Joy is still playing over the brown abyss.

Day of my life!
Toward evening it goes.
Already your eye
   glows half-broken,
already your dew's
   tear drops are welling,
already runs still over white seas
your love's purple,
your last hesitant blessedness.

III

Cheerfulness, golden one, come!
   you of death
the most secret and sweetest foretaste!
Did I run too rash on my way?
Only now that my foot has grown weary,
   your eye catches up with me,
   your *joy* catches up with me.

Round me but wave and play.
   Whatever was hard
sank into blue oblivion—
idle stands now my boat.
Storm and drive—how it forgot that!
   Wish and hope have drowned,
   smooth lie soul and sea.

Siebente Einsamkeit!
  Nie empfand ich
näher mir süße Sicherheit,
wärmer der Sonne Blick.
—Glüht nicht das Eis meiner Gipfel noch?
Silbern, leicht, ein Fisch,
schwimmt nun mein Nachen hinaus. . .

Venedig

An der Brücke stand
jüngst ich in brauner Nacht.
Fernher kam Gesang:
goldener Tropfen quolls
über die zitternde Fläche weg.
Gondeln, Lichter, Musik—
trunken schwamms in die Dämmrung hinaus. . .

Meine Seele, ein Saitenspiel,
sang sich, unsichtbar berührt,
heimlich ein Gondellied dazu,
zitternd vor bunter Seligkeit.
—Hörte jemand ihr zu? . . .

Vereinsamt

  Die Krähen schrein
Und ziehen schwirren Flugs zur Stadt:
  Bald wird es schnein.—
Wohl dem, der jetzt noch—Heimat hat!

  Nun stehst du starr,
Schaust rückwärts, ach! wie lange schon!

Seventh loneliness!
  Never felt I
nearer me sweet security,
warmer the sun's eye.
Does not the ice of my peaks still glow?
  Silver, light, a fish,
    my bark now swims out.

Walter Kaufmann

Venice

At the bridge of late
I stood in the brown night.
From afar came a song:
as a golden drop it welled
over the quivering surface.
Gondolas, lights, and music—
drunken it swam out into the twilight.

My soul, a stringed instrument,
sang to itself, invisibly touched,
a secret gondola song,
quivering with iridescent happiness.
—Did anyone listen to it?

Walter Kaufmann

The Solitary

Harsh cry the crows
And townward take their whirring flight;
Soon comes the snows—
Happy who has a home this night.

With glances dead
Thou gazest backward as of old!

Was bist du Narr
Vor Winters in die Welt entflohn?

Die Welt—ein Tor
Zu tausend Wüsten stumm und kalt!
Wer das verlor,
Was du verlorst, macht nirgends halt.

Nun stehst du bleich,
Zur Winterwanderschaft verflucht,
Dem Rauche gleich,
Der stets nach kältern Himmeln sucht.

Flieg, Vogel, schnarr
Dein Lied im Wüstenvogel-Ton!—
Versteck, du Narr,
Dein blutend Herz in Eis und Hohn!

Die Krähen schrein
Und ziehen schwirren Flugs zur Stadt:
Bald wird es schnein.—
Weh dem, der keine Heimat hat!

Sternen-Moral

Vorausbestimmt zur Sternenbahn,
Was geht dich, Stern, das Dunkel an?

Roll selig hin durch diese Zeit!
Ihr Elend sei dir fremd und weit!

Der fernsten Welt gehört dein Schein:
Mitleid soll Sünde für dich sein!

Nur *ein* Gebot gilt dir: sei rein!

Why hadst thou fled
Unto the world from winter's cold?

The world—a gate
To freezing deserts dumb and bare!
Who lost what late
Thou lost is homeless everywhere.

Pale one, to bleak
And wintry pilgrimages driven,
Smoke-like to seek
The ever colder heights of heaven.

Soar, bird, fling wide
That song of birds in deserts born!
O madman, hide
Thy bleeding heart in ice and scorn.

Harsh cry the crows
And townward take their whirring flight;
Soon come the snows—
Woe unto him who has no home this night.

Ludwig Lewisohn

Star Morals

Unto a heavenly course decreed,
Star, of the darkness take no heed.

Roll onward through this time and range!
Its woe to thee be far and strange!

To utmost worlds thy light secure:
No pity shall thy soul endure!

But one command is thine: be pure!

Ludwig Lewisohn

Dem unbekannten Gott

Noch einmal, eh ich weiterziehe
und meine Blicke vorwärts sende,
heb ich vereinsamt meine Hände
zu dir empor, zu dem ich fliehe,
dem ich in tiefster Herzenstiefe
Altäre feierlich geweiht,
daß allezeit
mich deine Stimme wieder riefe.

Darauf erglüht tiefeingeschrieben
das Wort: Dem unbekannten Gotte.
Sein bin ich, ob ich in der Frevler Rotte
auch bis zur Stunde bin geblieben:
sein bin ich—und ich fühl die Schlingen,
die mich im Kampf darniederziehn
und, mag ich fliehn,
mich doch zu seinem Dienste zwingen.

Ich will dich kennen, Unbekannter,
du tief in meine Seele Greifender,
mein Leben wie ein Sturm Durchschweifender,
du Unfaßbarer, mir Verwandter!
Ich will dich kennen, selbst dir dienen.

Unverzagt

Wo du stehst, grab' tief hinein!
Drunten ist die Quelle!
Lass die dunklen Männer schrein:
„Stets ist drunten—Hölle!"

To the Unknown God

Once more before I wander on
and turn my eyes to distant lands,
in solitude I raise my hands
to you on high to whom I fly,
whom in my heart's profundity
I hallowed altars to implore
that evermore
your voice might call again to me.

On them is glowing, inscribed deep,
the word: Unto the Unknown God.
His am I, although in the sinners' squad
until this hour I did keep:
his am I, and I feel the chains
that in my fight I can't untie
and, though I fly,
force me to serve the god again.

I want to know you, Unknown One,
you that are reaching deep into my soul
and ravaging my life, a savage gale,
you Inconceivable and yet Related One!
I want to know you—even serve.

Walter Kaufmann

Undaunted

Where you stand, dig deep and pry!
Down there is the well.
Let the obscurantists cry:
"Down there's only—hell!"

Walter Kaufmann

Index

GERMAN

ENGLISH

ACKNOWLEDGMENTS

Every reasonable effort has been made to locate the parties who hold rights to previously published translations reprinted here. We gratefully acknowledge permission to reprint material from the following publications:

From *A Collection of German Poetry,* trans. Gerd Gillhoff (1973): Eichendorff, "Conversation in the Forest"; Hebbel, "Image of Autumn"; Keller, "In the City" I; Lenau, "The Three"; and Storm, "The Seashore." Reprinted by permission of Gerd Gillhoff.

From *A German Garden of the Heart,* trans. John E. Rothensteiner (B. Herder Book Co., St. Louis, 1934): Storm, "Regine." Reprinted by permission of Tan Books & Publishers, Inc.

Alcaic Poems by Friedrich Hölderlin, trans. Elizabeth Henderson (Frederick Ungar Publishing Co., New York, 1963): "Go down, fair sun. . . ." Reprinted by permission of Frederick Ungar Publishing Co.

From *An Anthology of German Poetry from Hölderlin to Rilke in English Translation,* ed. Angel Flores (Doubleday Anchor Books, New York, 1965): Brentano, "Serenade," trans. Herman Salinger; Droste-Hülshoff, "The Pond," trans. Herman Salinger; Eichendorff, "Evening," trans. Edwin Morgan; Eichendorff, "Nocturne," trans. Herman Salinger; Heine, "I dreamt the old, old dream anew," trans. Herman Salinger; Mörike, "In Spring," trans. Vernon Watkins; and Platen-Hallermünde, "The Pilgrim at St. Yuste," trans. Edwin Morgan. Reprinted by permission of Angel Flores.

From *Anthology of German Poetry Through the Nineteenth Century,* ed. Alexander Gode and Frederick Ungar, 2nd rev. ed. (Frederick Ungar Publishing Co., New York, 1972): Brentano, "The Spinstress' Song," trans. Alexander Gode; Claudius, "Evening Song," trans. Alexander Gode, "The Stargazing Maiden," trans. Sheema

Z. Buehe, and "A Song of War," trans. Albert Bloch; Eichendorff, "Divining Rod," trans. Allison Turner, and "Night," trans. Isabel S. MacInnes; Hölderlin, "Half of Life," trans. Willard R. Trask and Alexander Gode; Keller, "See there the star," trans. Alexander Gode; Lenau, "Plea," trans. G. C. Schoolfield; Mörike, "Fair Rohtraut," trans. Isabel S. MacInnes; and Schiller, "The Gifts of Fortune" and "Nenia," trans. Alexander Gode. Reprinted by permission of Frederick Ungar Publishing Co.

From *A Treasury of German Ballads,* ed. Helen Kurz Roberts (Frederick Ungar Publishing Co., New York, 1964): Fontane, "The Bridge on the Tay," trans. Helen Kurz Roberts. Reprinted by permission of Frederick Ungar Publishing Co.

Friedrich Hölderlin/Eduard Mörike: Selected Poems, trans. Christopher Middleton (University of Chicago Press, 1972): Hölderlin, "Hyperion's Song of Fate," "The Farewell" (2nd version), and "Remembrance"; Mörike, "To an Aeolian Harp," "Peregrina" I–IV, "Girl's First Love Song," "The Forsaken Girl," and "September Morning." Reprinted by permission of University of Chicago Press.

From *German Life and Letters* 11/4 (July 1958): Keller, "Evening Song," trans. K. W. Maurer. Reprinted by permission of Basil Blackwell Publisher.

From *German Verse from the Twelfth to the Twentieth Century in English Translation* by J. W. Thomas. Copyright 1964 The University of North Carolina Press. Published for Studies in the Germanic Languages and Literatures: Claudius, "Christiane" and "Death and the Girl"; Hölty, "To the Evening Star"; Rückert, "Barbarossa"; Storm, "July"; and Uhland, "Spring Faith." Reprinted by permission of The University of North Carolina Press.

From *Goethe: Selected Poems,* ed. Christopher Middleton. Copyright © 1983 by Suhrkamp/Insel Pubs. Boston, Inc. "A Song to Mahomet" and "Reunion," trans. Christopher Middleton; "Anacreon's Grace," "Sonnet," and "Blessed Longing," trans. Michael Hamburger. Copyright © 1982 by Michael Hamburger. Reprinted by permission of Suhrkamp/Insel Pubs. Boston Inc.

From *Heinrich Heine: Paradox and Poet* by Louis Untermeyer (Harcourt, Brace & Co., New York, 1937): "I wish that all my love-songs" and "The Asra." Reprinted by permission of Harcourt Brace Jovanovich.

Heinrich Heine: Selected Works, trans. and ed. Helen M. Mustard, poetry trans. Max Knight (Random House, New York, 1973): "A spruce is standing lonely" and "Memorial Day," trans. Max Knight. Reprinted by permission of Random House.

From *Hölderlin: Poems and Fragments,* trans. Michael Hamburger (Cambridge University Press, 1980): "The Ages of Life," "To the Fates," and "Diotima." Reprinted by permission of Cambridge Univeristy Press.

From *Poems and Letters of Nikolaus Lenau,* trans. Winthrop H. Root (Frederick Ungar Publishing Co., New York, 1964): "Loneliness" I–II. Reprinted by permission of Frederick Ungar Publishing Co.

From *Sappho to Valéry: Poems in Translation* by John Frederick Nims. Copyright © 1971 by John Frederick Nims (Rutgers University Press, 1971): Goethe, "May Song," "The Meeting, The Departure," "To the Moon," "Mignon," and "Permanence in Change." Reprinted by permission of John Frederick Nims.

From *The Complete Poems of Heinrich Heine: A Modern English Version* by Hal Draper. Copyright © 1982 by Hal Draper: "When I go past your window," "The Lotus flower is drooping," "From olden tales it flings out," and "Oh, once I had a lovely fatherland." Reprinted by permission of Suhrkamp/Insel Pubs. Boston Inc.

From *The Complete Poems of Heinrich Heine: A Modern English Version* by Hal Draper (Suhrkamp/Insel Pubs. Boston Inc., 1982): "When I go past your window," "The Lotus flower is drooping," "From olden tales it flings out," and "Oh, once I had a lovely fatherland." Reprinted by permission of Suhrkamp/Insel Pubs. Boston Inc.

From *The Eternal Feminine: Selected Poems of Goethe,* ed. Frederick Ungar (Frederick Ungar Publishing Co., New York, 1980): "Primeval Words, Orphic," trans. Max Knight and Joseph Fabry. Reprinted by permission of Frederick Ungar Publishing Co.

From *The Permanent Goethe,* ed. Thomas Mann (The Dial Press, New York, 1954): "Who Yearning Knows" and "The Gods Give Everything," trans. Stephen Spender. © 1954 by Stephen Spender. Reprinted by permission of Literistic Ltd.

From *Twenty German Poets,* ed. and trans. Walter Kaufmann (Modern Library, New York, 1962): Nietzsche, "The Sun Sinks" I–III, "Venice," "To the Unknown God," and "Undaunted." Reprinted by permission of Hazel D. Kaufmann.